WORKING TOGETHER FOR DEVELOPMENT RESULTS

LESSONS FROM ADB AND CIVIL SOCIETY ORGANIZATION ENGAGEMENT IN SOUTH ASIA

DECEMBER 2022

ASIAN DEVELOPMENT BANK

ADB

© 2022 Asian Development Bank
6 ADB Avenue, Mandaluyong City, 1550 Metro Manila, Philippines
Tel +63 2 8632 4444; Fax +63 2 8636 2444
www.adb.org

Some rights reserved. Published in 2022.

ISBN 978-92-9269-851-5 (print); 978-92-9269-852-2 (electronic); 978-92-9269-853-9 (ebook)
Publication Stock No. TCS220518
DOI: http://dx.doi.org/10.22617/TCS220518

The views expressed in this publication are those of the authors and do not necessarily reflect the views and policies of the Asian Development Bank (ADB) or its Board of Governors or the governments they represent.

ADB does not guarantee the accuracy of the data included in this publication and accepts no responsibility for any consequence of their use. The mention of specific companies or products of manufacturers does not imply that they are endorsed or recommended by ADB in preference to others of a similar nature that are not mentioned.

By making any designation of or reference to a particular territory or geographic area, or by using the term "country" in this document, ADB does not intend to make any judgments as to the legal or other status of any territory or area.

Please contact pubsmarketing@adb.org if you have questions or comments with respect to content, or if you wish to obtain copyright permission for your intended use that does not fall within these terms, or for permission to use the ADB logo.

Corrigenda to ADB publications may be found at http://www.adb.org/publications/corrigenda.

Notes:
In this publication, "$" refers to United States dollars.
All photos by ADB, unless otherwise stated.

On the cover: Civil society organizations and ADB work together for development results (photo by iStock.com).

Cover design by Nonie Villanueva.

Contents

Contents

Tables, Figures, and Box

Tables

Figures

Box

Abbreviations

ADB	Asian Development Bank
BBCP	Bagmati Beautification Concern Platform
BRM	Bangladesh Resident Mission
CBO	community-based organization
CMS	consultant management system
COVID-19	coronavirus disease
CPS	country partnership strategy
CSO	civil society organization
DMC	developing member country
DPOB	Disabled People's Organization of Bhutan
GAP	gender action plan
GESI	gender equality and social inclusion
HEAVEN	Health and Agriculture and Village Education Network (India)
IDS	Integrated Development Society Nepal
ISSC	industry sector skills council
JFPR	Japan Fund for Prosperous and Resilient Asia and the Pacific
MASM	Manavadhikar Samajik Manch (Human Rights, Social, and Administration Platform)
MFF	multitranche financing facility
MFI	microfinance institution
MOLHR	Ministry of Labour and Human Resources
NGO	nongovernment organization
NRM	Nepal Resident Mission
PHED	Public Health Engineering Department
PKSF	Palli Karma Sahayak Foundation
PWD	person with disability
PMU	project management unit
SARD	South Asia Department
SDG	Sustainable Development Goal
SEIP	Skills for Employment Investment Program (Bangladesh)
SFAC	small farmer agricultural cooperative
SMEs	small and medium-sized enterprises
TA	technical assistance
TVET	technical and vocational education and training
WMG	water management group

Foreword

Civil society has a deep understanding of grassroots issues and relationships with communities. Civil society organizations (CSOs) can provide important contributions to long-term investments of the Asian Development Bank (ADB) in eradicating poverty in Asia and the Pacific. It should therefore be unsurprising that ADB's South Asia Department (SARD) has regularly demonstrated high levels of civil society engagement in its portfolio.

Building upon the findings of the 2015 publication titled *How Does ADB Engage Civil Society Organizations in Its Operations? Findings of an Exploratory Inquiry in South Asia,* this new report examines ADB's engagement with CSOs across South Asia in recent years. This also supports evidence that ADB's engagement with civil society in South Asian countries remains strong.

To what do we owe this success, and how can we improve moving forward? The report demonstrates that SARD mainstreams civil society engagement throughout the project cycle, beginning at policy dialogue, and remains engaged through design, implementation, and up to evaluation. Consultations play a key part of this engagement, and ADB continues to explore new and innovative ways to engage citizens through new methods and technologies.

Moving forward, we will need to explore more ways to bring civil society and governments together as partners in new and innovative methods of participation. Most importantly, we will explore—in collaboration with CSOs and our government counterparts—ways to further expand partnerships to reach our shared development goals.

K. Yokoyama

Kenichi Yokoyama
Director General
South Asia Department
Asian Development Bank

Preface

Civil society organizations (CSOs) have unique strengths and have specialized knowledge of communities. CSOs have been performing critical roles in promoting good governance and are an invaluable ally in the fight against poverty. Importantly, they connect the voices of citizens with government and decisionmakers—resulting in better planned, better implemented, and better managed projects that contribute to stronger and healthier communities. I am delighted to present *Working Together for Development Results: Lessons from ADB and Civil Society Organization Engagement in South Asia.*

This report reflects the commitment of the Asian Development Bank (ADB) and its Strategy 2030 to strengthen collaboration with civil society and builds upon significant strides in the last year to update our approach to civil society through a suite of policy and guidance materials to assist our teams and government partners in operationalizing their engagement.

As part of this updated and strengthened approach to civil society engagement, ADB introduced a new corporate results indicator that looks at the civil society engagement planned at the start of each project and compares it to that which is delivered by project completion. It is upon this data that this report builds its findings.

Also offered in this report are thoughtful perspectives for those interested in improving the efficacy and sustainability of development operations more broadly. Citizens and CSOs must be engaged throughout the entire project life cycle—from policy to project design to monitoring and evaluation—and that their engagement is most effective when it is both early and often.

We are proud to be a strong and steadfast partner to the citizens, governments, and CSOs of Asia and the Pacific and to lead the way in working to continuously strengthen our approach on civil society engagement.

Bruno Carrasco
Director General concurrently
Chief Compliance Officer
Sustainable Development and
Climate Change Department
Asian Development Bank

Acknowledgments

This report was prepared for the Asian Development Bank (ADB) by the principal author and co-researcher, consultant Emma Walters. Consultant Jaime B. Antonio Jr. was co-researcher.

The work was completed under the supervision of Elaine Thomas, principal operations coordination specialist, (conflict-affected situations) of ADB's Sustainable Development and Climate Change Department (SDCC) and Francesco Tornieri, principal social development specialist of the South Asia Department (SARD), who provided invaluable oversight, guidance, and support.

Brenda Batistiana, SARD consultant; Puri Gamon, associate social development officer (gender), SARD; Rose Postrado Buenaventura, associate project analyst, SARD; and Palak Rawal and Xiaoming Zhong, SDCC consultants provided additional support and advice. Marina Best edited an earlier version of the report and provided additional inputs. Ma. Catherine Malilay supported the full report preparation and publication process.

The SARD CSO focal points in ADB's resident missions provided recommendations, inputs, and direction throughout the report process. These focal points were Gobinda Bar, senior external relations officer, Bangladesh Resident Mission; Nidup Tshering, senior social development officer (gender), Bhutan Resident Mission; Rajesh Kumar Deol, senior external relations officer, India Resident Mission; Binita Shah Khadka, senior external relations officer, Nepal Resident Mission; and H. D. Sudarshana A. Jayasundara, senior social development officer (gender), Sri Lanka Resident Mission.

Thanks to all these ADB team members and consultants for their guidance and inputs which helped bring this publication to completion.

A CSO Advisory Group provided additional independent input, support, and guidance for the publication. The group's members are as follows:
- Bangladesh: Maheen Sultan, senior fellow of practice and head of gender and social development cluster, BRAC Institute of Governance and Development
- Bhutan: Sonam Pem, executive director, Tarayana Foundation
- India: Prem Anand, general manager, Education and Health Projects, Hand in Hand India
- Maldives: Zameela Ahmed, country manager, Live and Learn Environmental Education Maldives
- Nepal: Sucheta Pyakuryal, director of the Centre for Governance, Institute for Integrated Development Studies
- Sri Lanka: Samitha Sugathimala, program director, Foundation for Innovative Social Development and South Asian regional coordinator of MenEngage

We sincerely thank the CSO Advisory Group members for their insights and review comments throughout the report.

Thanks also to many ADB and CSO staff, consultants, and others who generously gave their time and shared their knowledge with the researchers, either through participating in a survey, sharing their insights and knowledge in interviews, participating in study meetings, reviewing documents or contributing through other channels. Without their active participation, this work would not have been possible.

Executive Summary

Strategy 2030 is the long-term corporate strategy of the Asian Development Bank (ADB) that commits to strengthening its engagement with civil society organizations (CSOs).[1] Across South Asia, ADB is working closely with CSOs to deliver positive development results. ADB commissioned this report to

(i)   identify trends and changes in ADB's approaches to civil society engagement in the South Asia Department (SARD) and provide analysis;
(ii) identify recent SARD projects that have used or are using promising, innovative, or conventional approaches successfully yielding high levels of engagement to promote civil society engagement in ADB operations;
(iii) extract lessons from cases when the desired CSO engagement outcome was not achieved; and
(iv) provide insights into approaches used by SARD to engage with CSOs.[2]

The team examined SARD's approved projects (2015–2021), which planned to engage with CSOs, surveyed ADB SARD staff on the work they undertook with CSOs, and conducted a "deep dive" using key informant interviews with ADB and CSO staff and desk research focusing on 25 selected projects and three country partnership strategies (CPS).

Findings

The report identified that SARD leads ADB's regional departments in planning and delivering on planned CSO engagement and has a markedly higher proportion of projects delivering on CSO engagement plans than ADB overall. SARD performed significantly better than the ADB average on planning and delivering CSO engagement in its sovereign portfolio. In 2021, of ADB's regional departments, SARD had the highest proportion of projects that planned meaningful CSO engagement and the highest number of projects that delivered on these CSO engagement plans. Within SARD, the Nepal portfolio is leading the way in planning the highest levels of CSO engagement in its projects.

Most planned CSO engagement is through consultation with CSOs during project implementation, although a high proportion (approximately 38%) is through planned CSO engagement where the CSO implements a project component. Other areas where ADB engages CSOs in SARD are as beneficiaries or target groups by working with them to raise awareness, establishing community-based organizations (CBOs), and building their capacity as well as those of water user associations and farmer groups. A small proportion of planned CSO engagement includes CSOs taking an advocacy role or engaging in monitoring and evaluation.

---

[1]   ADB. 2018. *Strategy 2030: Achieving a Prosperous, Inclusive, Resilient, and Sustainable Asia and the Pacific*. Manila, para. 108; discussion of the terminology "civil society organizations" and "CSOs" is in page 3.
[2]   ADB's South Asia Department covers operations in six countries: Bangladesh, Bhutan, India, Maldives, Nepal, and Sri Lanka. For the purposes of this report, South Asia is considered these six ADB members.

In South Asia, project implementation with CSO engagement is performing well. Engagement with CSOs includes their participation as consultants, contractors, service providers, target groups, and beneficiaries. SARD is using conventional approaches to great effect. Examples include the use of local CSOs for assistance in safeguards delivery and gender action plan (GAP) and gender equality and social inclusion (GESI) action plan implementation and continued engagement with private sector representative CSOs such as chambers of commerce and industry associations.

SARD is adopting tailored approaches to enhance CSO engagement in the preparation of CPS. Country teams are customizing approaches to CPS preparation to suit local circumstances. In Nepal, CPS consultations engaged CSOs from across the country to ensure a range of voices were heard, including excluded and vulnerable groups.[3] Online consultations in Bangladesh expanded the reach of CSO engagement in CPS preparation.

Robust CSO engagement leads to improved project design. In Sri Lanka, advocacy CSO inputs during project design led to stronger environmental protection measures on a renewable energy project. In the Maldives, CSO inputs during project preparation strengthened the gender dimensions of a project's design.

CSOs perform a range of roles in coordination and capacity development during project implementation in South Asia. In Bangladesh, industry associations play a multifaceted role in project implementation, including coordination and capacity development as partners on a project focusing on skills development. In Sri Lanka, a case study demonstrates how collaboration enhances a local CSO's capacity to perform essential community coordination roles. A case study from Nepal shows how networks of grassroots CSOs are powerful instruments for wide-scale community coordination activities and can work with communities to generate high levels of community ownership and sustainable project interventions, thus increasing impact.

CSOs offer innovative strategies and approaches that strengthen project implementation. The report examines projects from India, the Maldives, and Sri Lanka to demonstrate the special CSO initiatives that SARD uses to strengthen project implementation. One case study demonstrates how CSOs act as a bridge among project stakeholders to deliver innovative outcomes on a water project in India. Another case study from the Maldives explains how CSOs apply tailored community behavioral change approaches. Another case study shows how CSOs work closely with private sector stakeholders to optimize project impact.

CSOs are active in social service delivery during the implementation of ADB projects in South Asia. Three projects highlight how the niche expertise that CSOs offer is highly effective for social service delivery, particularly for increasing inclusion. The report finds that CSOs' close links to communities make them excellent partners for community-based social service delivery. One project in this section examines how microfinance CSOs provided a novel and sustainable financing model for livelihood restoration in an emergency.

Many CSOs are uniquely placed to assist in delivering social safeguards plan implementation because of their strong community relations and their understanding of local norms and community presence. The report demonstrates how CSOs help governments implement the safeguards, GAPs, and GESI action plans of ADB-financed loans and grants in South Asia.[4] Successful implementation of safeguards, GAPs, and GESI action plans are critical to project success. This work has a human element for which CSOs are particularly well-suited, due to their engagement with communities.

---

3   The terms "excluded" and "vulnerable" are defined in the discussion of the SARD gender equality and social inclusion framework at page 48.
4   Throughout this report, the term "ADB-financed" includes ADB-assisted, ADB-administered, and wholly ADB-financed operations.

ADB has committed to strengthening its engagement with CSOs. Across South Asia, ADB is working closely with CSOs to deliver positive development results.

CSOs are involved as early as possible as target groups or beneficiaries, which can increase the sustainability of a project and lead to better development outcomes. For example, one case study shows how CSOs as target groups may offer a direct link to hard-to-reach project beneficiaries at the community level. In Bangladesh, SARD is working with CBOs and using participatory approaches in water projects to support long-term sustainable and effective water management. The report also showcases a project which demonstrates that working with CSO microfinance institutions enhances community access to enterprise financing, training, and marketing support.

Technical assistance with CSO engagement is particularly appropriate for projects focusing on engagement with excluded and vulnerable communities. Technical assistance (TA) provides ADB with opportunities to pilot initiatives or demonstration activities with CSOs, which can be incorporated into the loan or grant, if the initiative or activity proves successful. For example, the report examines how, under TA, CSOs are providing unique perspectives to help ADB focus on male engagement in gender equality and women's empowerment, and how CSOs helped shape SARD's GESI framework. Another case study examines how innovative CSO models can be tested at scale through pilot and demonstration activities under ADB's TA.

In South Asia, there is an opportunity to increase CSO engagement in monitoring and evaluation and policy dialogue. The report notes that CSO engagement in monitoring ADB-financed operations in South Asia presents an opportunity for SARD and ADB to strengthen CSO engagement. Another opportunity for strengthening CSO engagement in SARD is upstream planning, particularly policy dialogue.

ADB has committed to strengthening collaboration with civil society organizations, with particular focus on operations that use grassroots participatory approaches to target poor and vulnerable groups and mobilize women and young people.

Lessons

Early CSO engagement leads to meaningful engagement and other benefits. One of the strongest themes to emerge from this report is the need to engage CSOs early in project preparation. Improved development outcomes and positive design changes can arise from CSO engagement, including with advocacy- and identity-based CSOs.

CSO engagement in monitoring and evaluation and upstream policy dialogue is a missed opportunity. The team did not find significant evidence of CSO engagement in monitoring and evaluation in SARD and notes an opportunity for increased regional engagement on policy dialogue. The nature of CSOs, particularly how these organizations use culturally sensitive approaches to improve citizens' lives, places them in a unique position to ensure that a diverse array of citizen voices is heard.

Building ADB and government skills in identifying CSOs and conducting due diligence will benefit projects. The report finds that ADB SARD staff need support with identifying appropriate CSOs plus conducting due diligence and financial assessments of CSOs for potential engagement. Project teams also need additional support to enhance meaningful CSO engagement.

Developing CSO capacity selectively is required for more effective engagement with ADB. Report respondents indicated that CSOs need to engage with ADB and government teams more effectively. CSOs' understanding of ADB's business model, procurement methods, and project cycles may be limited. Selective CSO capacity development is needed to increase the effectiveness of their engagement with ADB.

Raising awareness about existing flexible options for CSO procurement will improve procurement outcomes. Several ADB staff interviewed and surveyed mentioned the lack of specialized recruitment and contracting processes for CSO engagement. The report finds that ADB needs to consider raising awareness among ADB staff and government officials about the flexible options that already exist for CSO engagement and encourage staff and project teams to use the most suitable method for their project requirements.

Budgets for CSO activities and engagement can be inadequate and affect results. The report highlights that inadequate budgets were sometimes allocated for CSO activities, which has led to quality concerns about CSO deliverables. Budgets for CSO activities must be realistic in terms of what is expected.

Gaps remain between engineering and community engagement activities. In some projects, there appears to be a gap in understanding between project engineering staff and the CSOs performing community engagement activities. Often, participants said this gap narrows once the CSO starts work and the project staff see the value the CSO brings, particularly in resolving local conflicts and complaints.

Clear documentation of CSO roles in project documents results in better outcomes. Scoping CSOs during project design leads to clarity around CSO roles in project documents and minimizes misunderstandings on all sides during project implementation. ADB and government agencies can reduce misunderstandings by involving CSOs earlier in the project design and documenting roles well. ADB must ensure CSO roles are well-documented and expectations clearly detailed, particularly in terms of reference and consultation and participation plans.

CSOs need support to learn ADB and government processes. Some ADB staff reported challenges related to CSOs' lack of understanding of ADB or government policies and processes. This extended from procurement through to project implementation. Orienting CSOs on these policies and processes can be part of CSO capacity development from the outset. This issue requires specialist training and attention to acclimatizing CSOs to these policies and processes at the point of procurement.

Government–CSO project collaboration results in stronger relations and mutual understanding. ADB staff and CSO representatives raised a concern that occasionally government staff hesitate to engage CSOs on projects. Participants reported these issues often subsided once the project got underway and the CSO demonstrated its capability and worth to the project. This highlights how CSO engagement early in the project would be useful, and the need to encourage regular interaction among ADB, CSOs, and the government.

Recommendations

1. Invest in early CSO engagement. The findings indicate that more meaningful engagement of CSOs at the project design stage is needed, as this will lead to improved CSO participation during project implementation. A TA facility may be an ideal vehicle to ensure effective, productive, and sustainable partnerships among government, ADB, and CSOs. A TA facility would allow for scoping CSO engagement as consultants, service providers, and partners at the design stage, and assist governments through capacity development actions to sustainably engage with CSOs. Engaging advocacy- and identity-based CSOs in South Asia is a particular area where ADB could increase its investment in early engagement with CSOs.

2. Enhance CSO knowledge on ADB and government procurement and contracting processes. The report recommends training CSOs on using ADB's Consultant Management System and ADB and government procurement and contracting processes. In addition, ADB should consider (i) utilizing innovative procurement methods for CSOs; (ii) avoiding the least-cost selection method for procurement of CSOs unless the assignment is genuinely standard, small, and routine; (iii) using output-based contracts for CSOs and ensuring that adequate funds are advanced for CSOs to conduct project activities; and (iv) ensuring clear documentation of CSO roles in project planning documents.

3. Increase CSO roles in monitoring and evaluation. CSOs could be engaged to monitor aspects of ADB-financed projects, such as GAP or GESI action plan implementation or for results-based lending and verification of disbursement-linked indicators. ADB should provide support to CSOs to fulfill the roles of providing third-party monitoring of ADB-financed loans, grants, and TA. CSOs often use participatory approaches and simple tools to monitor service delivery including social audits, citizen report cards, digital storytelling, and citizen dashboards. These approaches have the added benefit of increasing citizen engagement in monitoring government service delivery. ADB project teams should assess CSOs' monitoring capacity and budget for their capacity development (particularly in areas such as data analysis or technology-heavy approaches) and involvement in these roles.

4. Encourage regular interaction among CSOs, ADB, and the government at country level, outside the project cycle. There is a need to enhance relationships among ADB, CSOs and governments, including more effectively bringing CSO specialist knowledge into ADB. Forming country-level ADB–government–CSO tripartite sector groups if nonexistent, or a CSO country advisory group for the ADB resident mission, will go a long way to CSOs getting to know ADB and the government, and vice versa. In addition, invite CSOs to present their experience at ADB and government planning events to allow government officials and ADB staff to identify which CSOs have the capacities they need and could add value to ADB-financed projects. Good practice and knowledge sharing are benefits of encouraging this tripartite interaction. ADB can play a strategic role in encouraging this engagement among ADB, government, and CSOs.

5. Increase the engagement of CSOs in upstream policy dialogue. ADB should conduct comprehensive stakeholder mapping in the early stages of policy formulation or review, prepare clear consultation plans with stakeholders, and share these in advance. ADB should share the draft policies or draft CPS before consultations, translated into appropriate national languages, with ample time for sharing comments so stakeholders can make meaningful and specific comments on proposals. During online consultations, CSOs from specific regions are often not convened together, as consultations focus on topics, not geographic proximity; however, ADB should also consider how CSOs may contribute to the policy dialogue process beyond seeking their inputs as key stakeholders.

Collectively, these recommendations build on the work that ADB is undertaking to enhance CSO engagement across South Asia and the broader Asia and Pacific region. By working with CSOs in ways they can appreciate and adapt to, ADB can facilitate CSOs' meaningful contributions to ADB's vision for a prosperous, inclusive, resilient, and sustainable Asia and the Pacific.

1

Introduction and Scope of the Report

In 2015, the South Asia Department (SARD)[1] of the Asian Development Bank (ADB) undertook a study to explore how civil society organizations (CSOs) are engaged in ADB-financed operations in South Asia.[2] The results show that ADB and its developing member countries (DMCs) engage CSOs in a variety of ways throughout the project cycle and concluded that the most common engagement modality was through ADB and member governments contracting CSOs like they would for-profit consulting firms to deliver specific services during a project.

In 2020, ADB introduced a new approach to measuring its engagement with CSOs by revising an engagement tracking indicator in ADB's corporate results framework. Rather than reporting on what level of CSO engagement was planned in ADB sovereign operations, the new engagement indicator committed ADB to reporting on the proportion of planned, meaningful CSO engagement delivered at project completion (see Appendix 1 for more detail).

SARD had the highest number of projects with planned and delivered CSO engagement in an analysis prepared by ADB's Nongovernment Organization (NGO) and Civil Society Center for reporting on the ADB's Development Effectiveness Review for 2020.

---

[1] ADB's South Asia Department covers operations in six countries: Bangladesh, Bhutan, India, Maldives, Nepal, and Sri Lanka.

[2] ADB. 2015. *How Does ADB Engage Civil Society Organizations in Its Operations? Findings of an Exploratory Inquiry in South Asia.* Manila. Throughout this report, the term "ADB-financed" includes ADB-assisted, ADB-administered, and wholly ADB-financed operations.

What was SARD doing to deliver these positive results on CSO engagement? Did it use any special or innovative approaches? What could teams within SARD and across ADB, member governments, and CSOs learn from this experience?

The objectives of this report are the following:

(i) Identify trends and changes in ADB's approaches to civil society engagement in SARD and provide analysis.

(ii) Identify recent SARD projects that have used or are using promising, innovative, or conventional approaches successfully yielding high levels of engagement to promote civil society engagement in ADB operations.

(iii) Extract lessons from cases when the desired civil society engagement outcome was not achieved.

(iv) Provide insights into approaches used by SARD to engage with CSOs.

Methodology. The methodology involved these steps:

(i) Form a project steering committee comprising staff from SARD and NGO and Civil Society Center plus the staff responsible for facilitating CSO engagement in the ADB resident missions in SARD countries.[3]

(ii) Establish a CSO Advisory Group for the publication with one CSO representative from each of the six SARD countries to advise the team.

(iii) Conduct a desk review of project documents to determine planned CSO engagement trends within SARD during 2015–2021.

(iv) Survey SARD staff to determine the type of CSOs SARD engages with, their areas of expertise, projects with innovative approaches to CSO engagement, and any lessons or advice from SARD staff on working with CSOs.

(v) List projects, country partnership strategies (CPS), and policies to be examined through key informant interviews and the CSO engagement planned, delivered, or being delivered.

(vi) Undertake key informant interviews with ADB staff and selected CSOs to explore CSO engagement in greater depth and distill specific approaches and lessons.

(vii) Synthesize reviews by SARD and NGO and Civil Society Center staff and the CSO Advisory Group.

The list of projects involved in this report is in Appendix 2. The list of people interviewed is in Appendix 3.

Limitations. There are several limitations of this report:

(i) Due to the coronavirus disease (COVID-19) pandemic, the report undertook all investigations through online interviews, limiting researchers' ability to engage with interviewees.

(ii) While the team engaged with ADB staff and a limited number of CSOs, they did not interview executing or implementing agency staff because the main objective of the report was to determine ADB's approaches to civil society engagement. Interviews with government staff, which were not part of the report, may have provided additional lessons.

---

3   Staff responsible for CSO engagement at the resident missions in SARD are called "CSO focals."

(iii)   While the report showcases good examples of innovation or successful engagement with CSOs, it is not a comprehensive examination of all projects approved during the period and thus does not cover all forms of engagement nor all examples of good or ineffective practice.

(iv)   The team examined projects conducted between 2015–2021 and sought to review projects approved from 2015 onwards. However, some projects were continuations of earlier projects, particularly projects that received additional financing. In these cases, the earlier project (pre-2015) is briefly discussed to give some context to the work done from 2015 to the present. The report mentions a few projects not yet approved but in the pipeline.

(v)   The project team focused exclusively on ADB sovereign operations since CSO engagement in nonsovereign operations is limited.

Terminology. ADB uses the following definition of civil society organizations:

The term "civil society organization" refers generically to organizations (i) not based in government, and (ii) not created to earn profit. ADB defines CSOs as nonprofit organizations independent from the government, which operate around common interests. They vary in size, interests, and function and include nongovernment organizations (NGOs), youth groups, community-based organizations, independent academic and research institutes, professional associations, foundations, faith-based organizations, people's organizations, and labor unions. CSOs represent the interests of their members or others.[4]

In South Asia, the term "nongovernment organization" (NGO) is more commonly used than "civil society organization." NGOs are a subset of CSOs and do not include organizations like chambers of commerce, trade unions, and professional associations, which are also considered CSOs. This publication uses the terms NGO or community-based organization (CBO) where the project team or project documents refer to these entities in this way (or water user association or similar). In all other cases, the report uses the broader term "civil society organization" or CSO to cover the full range of entities that comprise this sector.

The context: Civil society organizations and the civic space in South Asia. The context for this report is the changing space for civil society globally. Despite the formalized engagement of CSOs in the achievement of the Sustainable Development Goals (SDGs), the specific role for CSOs in partnering on SDGs 16 and 17 and their active roles and participation in the other SDGs, the space for civil society has been categorized as "shrinking" or "closing."[5] Some argue this is not affecting all CSOs equally and is disproportionally affecting those

4   ADB. 2021. Promotion of Engagement with Civil Society Organizations. *Operations Manual.* OM E4. Manila. para. 2.
5   For example, a 2020 report by the South Asia Collective opens with "Across South Asia, civil society is being increasingly constrained." It recognizes several factors are having a restrictive effect on the operation of CSOs in South Asia: (i) restrictions on freedom of expression, particularly through repressive laws; (ii) contraction of rights to freedom of association, particularly through denying or revoking registration certificates for CSOs; (iii) restrictions on freedom of assembly; (iv) targeting religious minorities; (v) targeting human rights defenders; and (vi) restrictions on civil liberties as a result of the COVID-19 pandemic. South Asia Collective. 2020. *South Asia State of Minorities Report 2020. Minorities and Shrinking Civic Space.* Kathmandu: South Asia Collective.

with liberal, human rights perspectives, often aid-funded.[6] The COVID-19 pandemic may have further reduced the space in which CSOs, governments, and the private sector operate, although opportunities for some CSOs may have increased through previously unavailable options for virtual engagement. Many CSOs face increasing restrictions on their activities and their ability to freely operate within their home countries. Some CSOs face restrictive registration requirements, which may limit their ability to deliver services and engage in projects. It may be more effective to recognize that the space for civil society is uneven across CSO types, sectors, and regions and within states.

---

6   N. Hossain et al. 2018. What Does Closing Civic Space Mean for Development? A Literature Review and Proposed Conceptual Framework. *IDS Working Paper*. No. 515. Brighton, UK: Institute of Development Studies.

2

ADB's Commitment to Engagement with Civil Society Organizations

ADB will work with CSOs to tap their unique strengths, such as their local presence and specialized knowledge.

ADB's commitment to engage the civil society sector was first outlined at the corporate policy level in a 1987 policy paper "The Bank's Cooperation with Non-Governmental Organizations." Engagement with civil society was seen as an effective means of supplementing ADB's efforts in selected operational areas.[7] In 1998, ADB adopted the new policy "Cooperation Between the Asian Development Bank and Nongovernment Organizations" that outlined how "an expanded program of cooperation with NGOs in its member countries will be pursued" in "project, programming, or policy activities…and country-specific considerations" (footnote 7). It also noted that "ADB will continue to explore innovative approaches to cooperation with NGOs."

ADB's new long-term corporate strategy, Strategy 2030, in section X: Delivering Through a Stronger, Better and Faster ADB, outlines ADB's commitment to civil society engagement. It states:

> **Strengthening collaboration with civil society organizations.** ADB will work with CSOs to tap their unique strengths, such as their local presence and specialized knowledge. It will explore opportunities for increasing their involvement in the design and implementation of projects supported by ADB. Particular focus will be on operations that use grassroots participatory approaches to target the poor and vulnerable groups, mobilize women and young people, and monitor project

---

[7] ADB. 2004. *Cooperation Between Asian Development Bank and Nongovernment Organizations.* Manila. This document was published in March 2004 as a typeset version of the official policy paper approved by ADB's Board of Directors on 27 March 1998.

activities and outputs. ADB will also seek their input and advice on the review of major ADB policies.[8]

On 19 May 2021, ADB further strengthened its commitment to engage with CSOs by updating its Operations Manual Section E4, which provides the policy basis for its engagement with CSOs. It states, "ADB pursues an expanded program of engagement with CSOs, where appropriate, in its member countries, in consultation with the government, with a view to strengthen the effectiveness, sustainability, and quality of the development services ADB provides."[9]

The reference to ADB working with CSOs in consultation with governments is critical. ADB is a member-based organization, and its members are governments. The fundamental relationship for ADB is with its member governments. This point is expanded in OM E4 in a later paragraph: "The fundamental relationship between ADB and a government, as well as the sovereignty of governments, continues to be recognized."[10]

It is difficult to overstate the importance of this point because it has implications for ADB's relationships with CSOs. At the project and CPS levels, the openness of ADB's members to civil society engagement determines the relationships among ADB, the government, and CSOs. At the project level, for ADB grants and loans, the member governments procure and work with CSOs.[11] Therefore, ADB's depth of engagement with CSOs is influenced by the views of the government of the country in which it is working.

---

8   ADB. 2018. *Strategy 2030: Achieving a Prosperous, Inclusive, Resilient, and Sustainable Asia and the Pacific.* Manila, para. 108; discussion of the terminology "civil society organizations" and "CSOs" is on page 3.
9   Footnote 4, para. 5.
10 Footnote 4, para. 6.
11 Conversely, ADB technical assistance is administered by ADB to help member governments plan and implement projects and improve knowledge and regional cooperation.

3

Civil Society Organization Engagement in ADB Operations in South Asia, 2015–2021

SARD leads ADB's regional departments in planning and delivering on planned CSO engagement and has a markedly higher proportion of projects delivering on CSO engagement plans than ADB overall.

Desk Review

SARD leads ADB's regional departments in planning and delivering on planned CSO engagement and has a markedly higher proportion of projects delivering on CSO engagement plans than ADB overall. In 2021, SARD managed the largest proportion of ADB's sovereign portfolio (33%), compared to 26% for Southeast Asia department, 23% for Central and West Asia, 14% for East Asia, and 3% for the Pacific Department.[12] In 2021, SARD had the highest proportion of projects that planned meaningful CSO engagement and the highest number of projects that delivered on these meaningful CSO engagement plans, among regional departments.[13] In 2021, 50% of all ADB sovereign projects that published project completion reports had planned to deliver meaningful CSO engagement (51 out of 103 projects), of which 76% (39 of 51 projects) delivered the planned, meaningful CSO engagement as documented at project completion. However, in SARD, the percentage of projects with planned, meaningful CSO engagement was 76% (22 out of 29 projects), of which 82% (18 of 22 projects) were delivered at project completion (Figures 1 and 2). SARD performed significantly better than the ADB average on planning and delivering CSO engagement in its sovereign portfolio.

---

[12]   ADB. 2022. *Annual Portfolio Performance Report 2021*. Manila.
[13]   In 2021, the East Asia Department delivered on its meaningful CSO engagement plans in 86% of projects, while SARD was 82%. However, the 86% delivery for the East Asia Department was from a much lower base: only 7 projects planned meaningful CSO engagement in the East Asia Department, compared to SARD's 22 projects in the same year.

Figure 1: Percentage of Sovereign Projects with Planned Civil Society Organization Engagement Delivered by ADB's Regional Departments, 2021

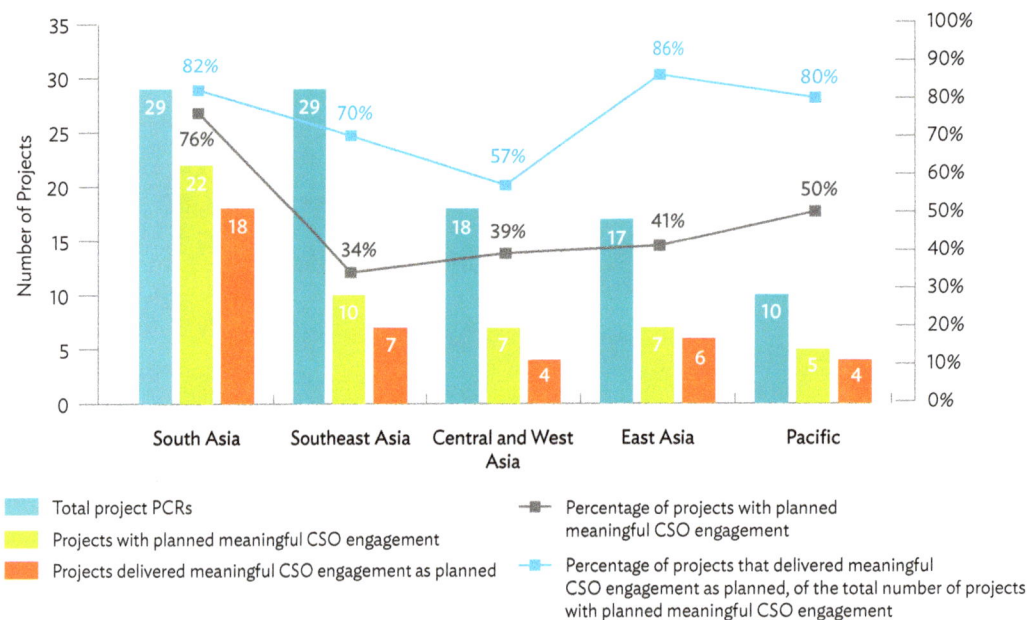

Legend:
- Total project PCRs
- Projects with planned meaningful CSO engagement
- Projects delivered meaningful CSO engagement as planned
- Percentage of projects with planned meaningful CSO engagement
- Percentage of projects that delivered meaningful CSO engagement as planned, of the total number of projects with planned meaningful CSO engagement

ADB = Asian Development Bank, CSO = civil society organization, PCR = project completion report.
Source: Asian Development Bank.

Figure 2: Number of Sovereign Projects with Planned Civil Society Organization Engagement Delivered by ADB's Regional Departments, 2021

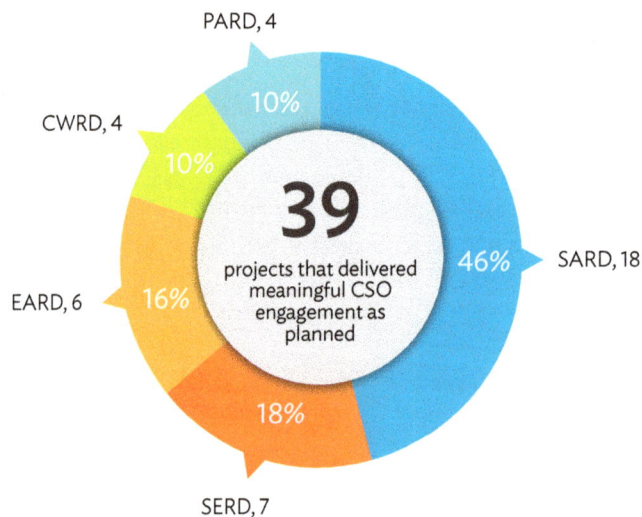

39 projects that delivered meaningful CSO engagement as planned

PARD, 4 — 10%
CWRD, 4 — 10%
EARD, 6 — 16%
SERD, 7 — 18%
SARD, 18 — 46%

ADB = Asian Development Bank, CSO = civil society organization, CWRD = Central and West Asia Department, EARD = East Asia Department, PARD = Pacific Department, SARD = South Asia Department, SERD = Southeast Asia Department.
Source: Asian Development Bank.

Project completion reports are approved after project completion so there is a significant lag between planning CSO activity and reporting. To obtain more recent data, the research team assessed all ADB SARD sovereign projects approved over 2015–2021 to determine the level of meaningful civil society engagement planned for SARD operations.

Thus, the data in Figures 3, 4, and 5, and Table 1 indicate only the planned CSO engagement, not delivered engagement. Figure 3 presents the results. Of 214 sovereign projects approved from 2015–2021 in SARD, 162 (76%) have planned meaningful civil society organization engagement.

Figure 3: Approved Sovereign Projects with Planned Meaningful Civil Society Organization Engagement by ADB's South Asia Department in 2015–2021

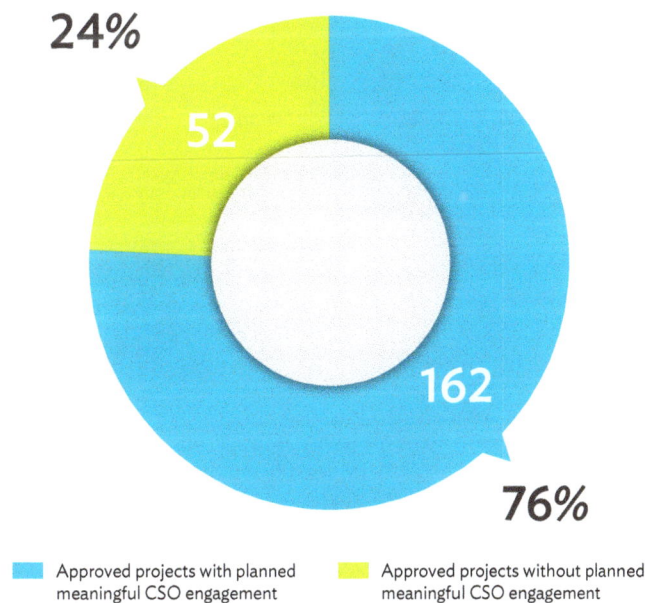

ADB = Asian Development Bank, CSO = civil society organization.
Source: Asian Development Bank.

Figure 4 presents the data for each of the six SARD countries. India has the highest number of projects overall and the highest number of projects with planned civil society engagement (63 out of 84, or 75%). ADB's ongoing sovereign portfolio in India, the largest in the Asia and Pacific region, includes 66 loans and 1 grant worth $15 billion.[14] Nepal has the highest percentage of projects with planned meaningful civil society engagement (21 projects out of 25 from 2015–2021, or 84%).

14   ADB. 2022. Member Fact Sheet: ADB's Work in India.

Figure 4: Approved Sovereign Projects with Planned Meaningful Civil Society Organization Engagement by ADB's South Asia Department in 2015–2021, by Country

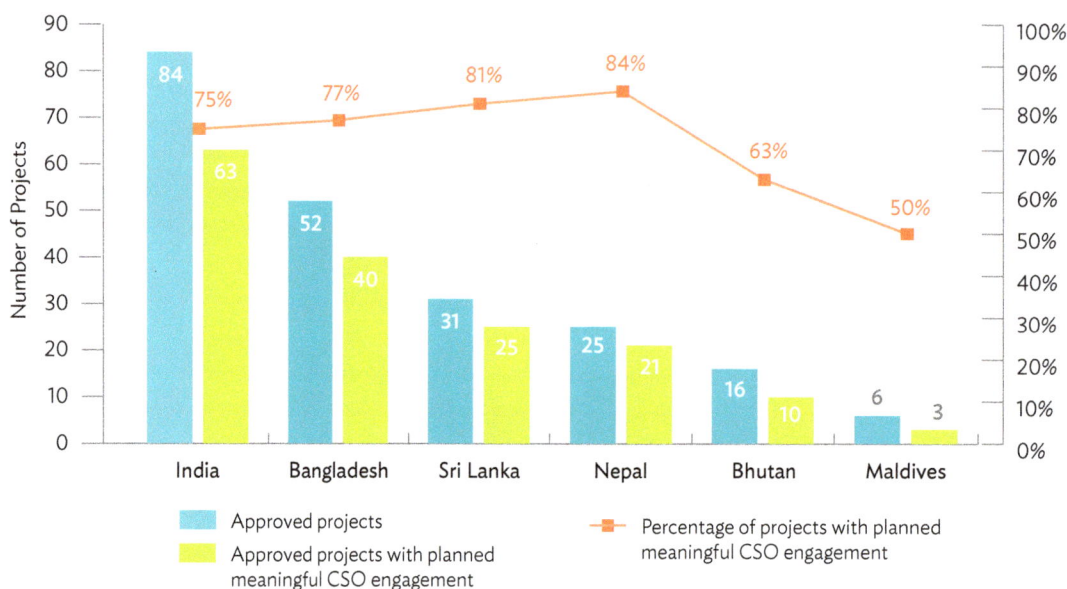

ADB = Asian Development Bank, CSO = civil society organization.
Source: Asian Development Bank.

Examination of the data by year (Figure 5) shows that the proportion of projects with planned meaningful civil society engagement remained relatively stable over 2015–2018, hovering around 82% of projects. However, 2019 saw a slight decline of planned meaningful engagement to 74% and in 2020 a more significant drop to 59%.[15] SARD reversed this decline in 2021, with 73% of projects that year planning meaningful engagement with CSOs. The explanation for the drop in planned meaningful CSO engagement in 2020 may have been the inability of ADB staff to work in the field due to the pandemic lockdowns and travel restrictions.

The team analyzed sectors of CSO engagement over 2015–2021. The highest proportion of SARD sovereign projects that had planned engagement were in water supply and sanitation (90%), education (89%), energy (86%), transport (85%), trade and industry (80%), agriculture and natural resources (75%), health (75%), and urban development (67%) sectors. Finally, the team analyzed the type of CSO engagement activity taking place within

---

15   The 2020 figure of 59% includes the five COVID-19 Pandemic Response Option loans approved in 2020. ADB processed these urgently with correspondingly low levels of planned civil society engagement. ADB processed these loans at speed as an emergency response to the COVID-19 pandemic early in 2020. The ADB Board approved the India COVID-19 Active Response and Expenditure Support Program (CARES) in April 2020 and the Bhutan, Bangladesh, and Nepal CARES programs in May 2020. The ADB Board approved the Maldives CARES Program in June 2020.

Figure 5: Approved Sovereign Projects with Planned Meaningful Civil Society Organization Engagement by ADB's South Asia Department in 2015–2021, by Year

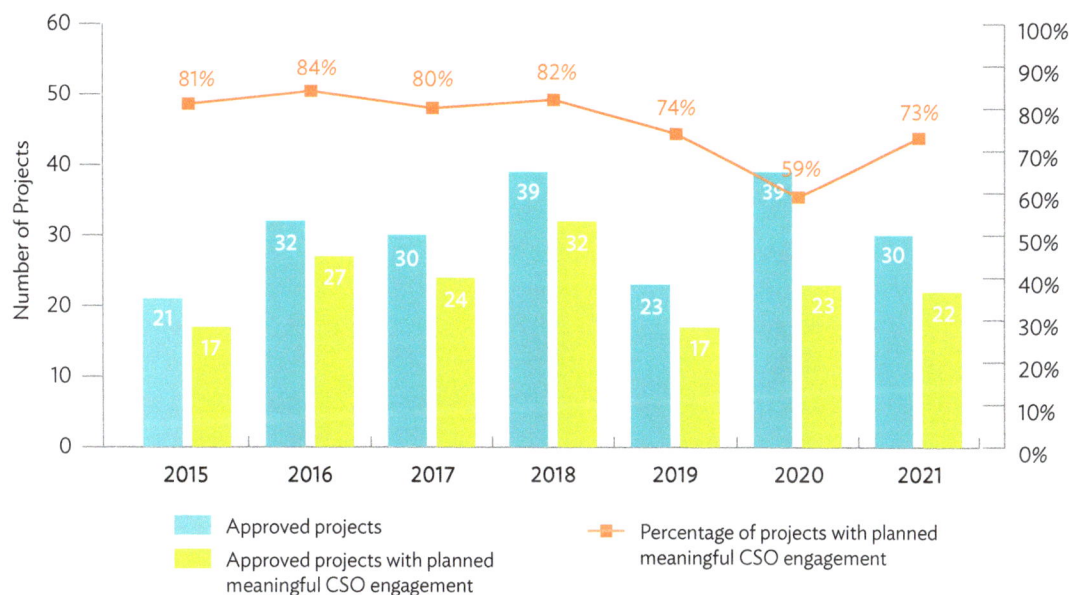

Approved projects
Approved projects with planned meaningful CSO engagement
Percentage of projects with planned meaningful CSO engagement

ADB = Asian Development Bank, CSO = civil society organization.
Source: Asian Development Bank.

SARD operations (Table 1). Most planned engagement happened through consultations with CSOs during project implementation. A high proportion of projects planned for CSOs to implement a project component or components.

Table 1: Planned Roles and Involvement of CSOs in 214 Sovereign Projects of ADB's South Asia Department, 2015–2021

Planned roles	No. of Projects
Participating in consultations during implementation	166
Implementing one or more project components	81
Project beneficiaries	65
Raising awareness	50
Training project beneficiaries	21
Developing CSO capacity	19
Involvement in advocacy	4

Note: Civil society organizations (CSOs) may have had more than one role in the 214 sovereign projects of ADB's South Asia Department taken into account for 2015–2021.
Source: Asian Development Bank.

TAKEAWAYS

- SARD leads ADB's regional departments in planning and delivering on planned CSO engagement and has a markedly higher proportion of projects delivering on CSO engagement plans than ADB overall.

- Within SARD, the Nepal portfolio is leading the way in planning the highest levels of CSO engagement in its projects.

- Most planned CSO engagement is through consultation with CSOs during project implementation, although a high proportion (approximately 38%) is through planned CSO engagement where the CSO implements a project component. Other areas where ADB engages CSOs in SARD are as beneficiaries or target groups and by working with them to raise awareness and develop CSOs such as CBOs, water user associations, and farmer groups for project purposes.

- A small proportion of planned CSO engagement includes CSOs taking an advocacy role or engaging in monitoring and evaluation.

- Planned meaningful CSO engagement in ADB-financed operations in South Asia remained steady from 2015–2018. It declined slightly in 2019, and dropped significantly in 2020, possibly due to the impact of the COVID-19 pandemic. This decline reversed in 2021.

ADB Staff Perceptions of Civil Society Organization Engagement: Survey Results

To further investigate these trends, the team surveyed ADB SARD staff. A total of 175 SARD staff were sent the survey from 21 June to 16 July 2021. The objective was to capture SARD staff experiences in engaging CSOs in ADB-financed projects, the types of CSOs the projects engaged, the CSO sector of activity, and any successful or innovative approaches and lessons in CSO engagement. The response rate was 57.7%, with 101 responses.

Figures 6, 7, and 8 show the type of CSOs engaged (or planned to be engaged), their sector focus, and the stage in the project cycle when the engagement took place or was planned. Most projects engaged with NGOs and CBOs, which mirrors the findings in the 2015 report. Staff reported low levels of CSO engagement with trade unions, peak or umbrella CSO networks, foundations, and advocacy- and identity-based CSOs.[16]

Figure 6: Survey Respondents Nominating Type of Civil Society Organizations Engaged or Planned to Be Engaged in ADB-Financed Projects, 2015–2020

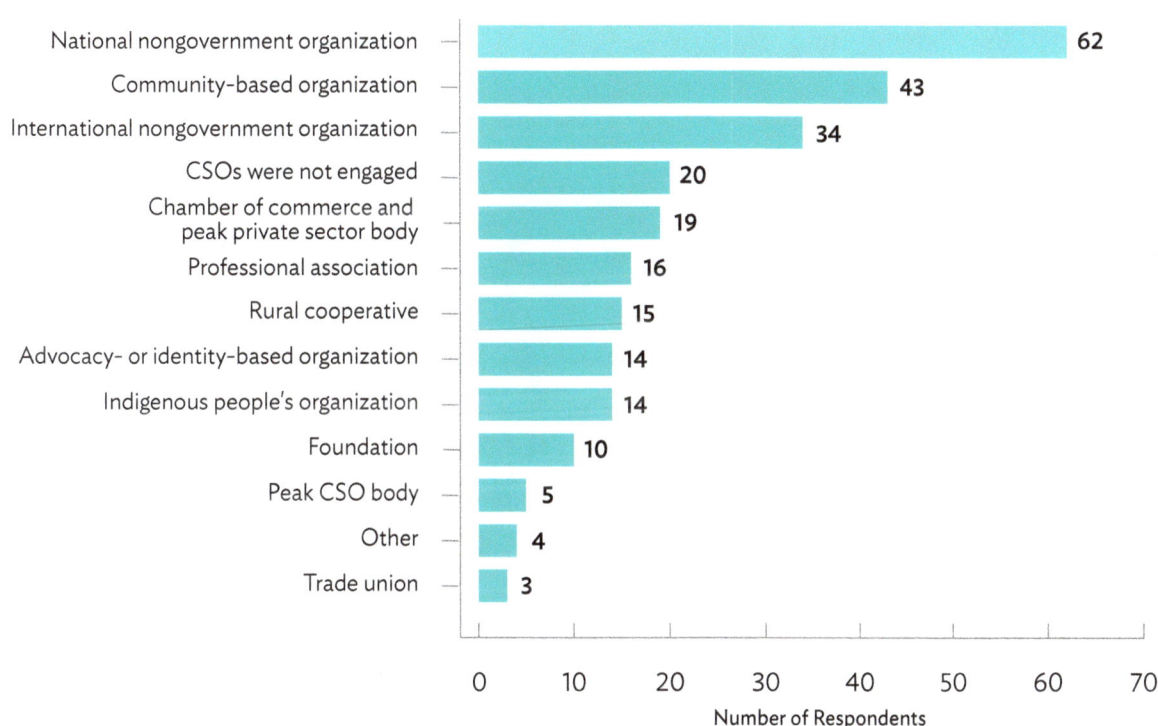

ADB = Asian Development Bank, CSO = civil society organization.
Source: Asian Development Bank.

The CSO areas of specialization are no surprise as these sectors typically include strong CSO activity and are similar to the sectors identified in the 2015 report. Agriculture and natural resources topped the list, followed closely by environmental and social safeguards, water supply and sanitation, gender equality, education and skills development, transport, urban development, social inclusion, and climate change and disaster risk management.

---

16 In ADB, advocacy organizations "engage in policy dialogue and other means to influence the views, policies, and actions of governments and other organizations and stakeholders such as ADB, the media and the community. They may also have an operational or service focus in addition to their advocacy focus or may work exclusively as advocacy organizations." Identity-based CSOs focus on the identity of the groups they represent, such as women, LGBT communities, persons with disabilities, caste-based CSOs, and others. This is an area where ADB could expand and deepen its engagement with CSOs.

Figure 7: Survey Respondents Indicating Areas of Specialization of Civil Society Organizations Engaged or Planned to be Engaged in ADB-Financed Projects, 2015–2020

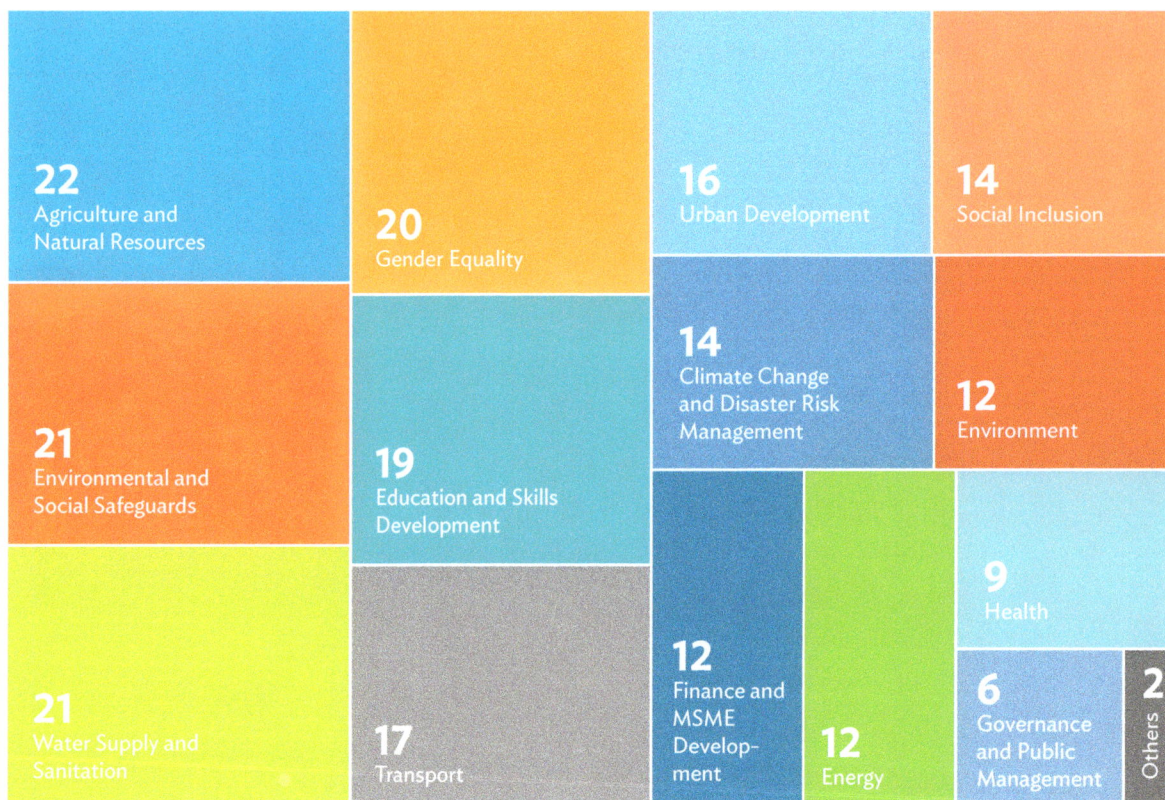

CSO = civil society organization, MSMEs = micro, small, and medium-sized enterprises.
Source: Asian Development Bank.

Figure 8 shows the point of engagement with CSOs in the project cycle as reported by ADB staff. Engagement mainly takes place during implementation, either in paid positions as consultants, contractors, or service providers, or in unpaid or voluntary roles, including project beneficiaries, target groups, or stakeholders. These findings mirror the 2015 report findings that most CSO engagement in South Asia was with CSOs as service providers or consultants.

The results show that CSO engagement in project design is relatively limited. Only one staff member reported a CSO playing a role in project evaluation. This indicates CSO engagement in project design, and engaging CSOs early, plus engaging CSOs in monitoring and evaluation, are areas where ADB and DMC governments could strengthen their CSO engagement and benefit from CSO expertise.

Figure 8: Survey Respondents Indicating Point of Engagement in the Project or Program Cycle of Civil Society Organizations Engaged or Planned to be Engaged in ADB-Financed Projects, 2015-2020

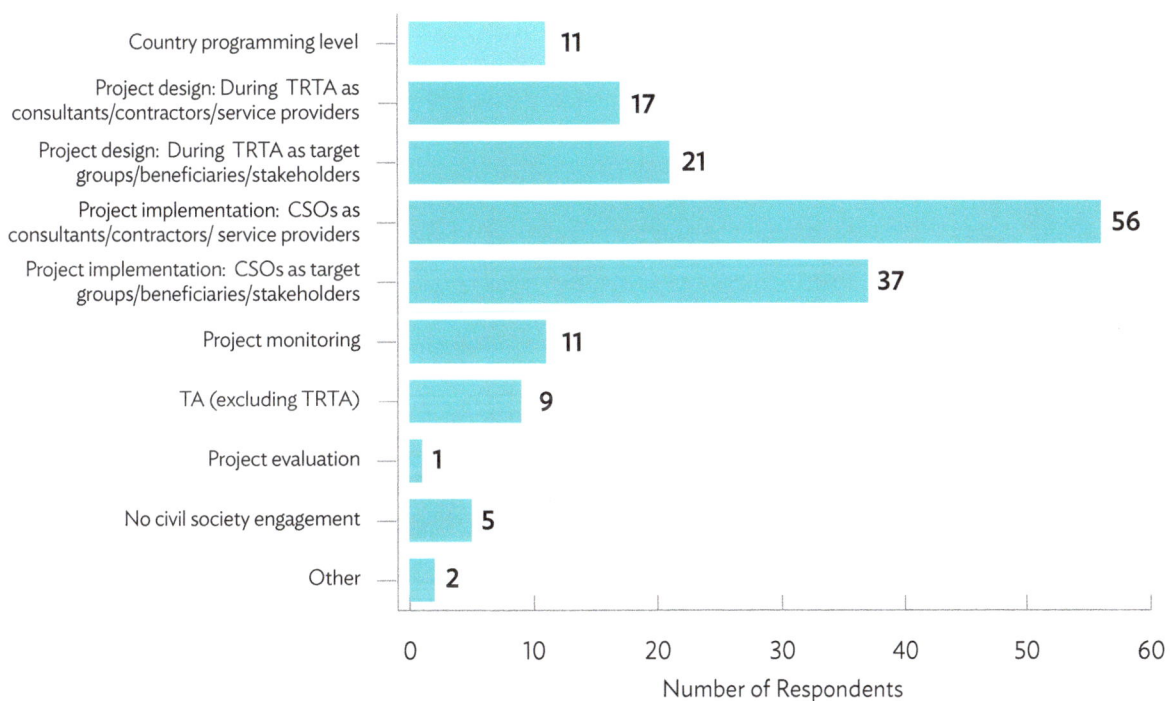

CSO = civil society organization, TA = technical assistance, TRTA = transaction TA.
Source: Asian Development Bank.

SARD staff were also asked to identify lessons or considerations for engaging with CSOs. These included the following:

(i) **CSO engagement strengthens both project design and implementation.** Staff pointed to specific design and implementation improvements resulting from CSO engagement.

(ii) **Engage CSOs early.** Engage CSOs early in the project preparation stage. Many survey respondents recommended earlier engagement and mentioned this second only to the value that CSOs bring to the development process.

(iii) **Due diligence and financial and capacity assessments.** Some respondents were concerned about how to conduct due diligence and financial and capacity assessments of CSOs. Identifying appropriate CSOs to play a role in ADB-financed operations is a related issue and ADB needs to address this gap.

(iv) **Resource CSO engagement.** An issue related to the lack of in-depth CSO engagement at the design phase is the inadequate budget sometimes allocated for CSO activities.

(v) **Clear documentation for CSOs.** Some survey respondents indicated there needed to be clearer documentation of CSO roles in the project planning documents.

(vi) **Reluctance to engage CSOs.** Some respondents indicated that some government agencies are unfamiliar with and occasionally reluctant to engage CSOs.

(vii) **Need for capacity development.** Many survey respondents indicated a need for capacity development for more effective CSO engagement, mainly strengthening CSO capacity to engage with ADB.

(viii) **Difficulties understanding processes and regulations.** Some ADB staff reported difficulties in CSOs not understanding ADB or government processes and regulations. This extended from procurement through to project implementation.

4

Case Studies of Civil Society Organization Engagement in the Project Cycle

Consulting widely and ensuring CSOs representing excluded and vulnerable people are included ensures the country programming strategy considers voices from all levels of society.

This section presents a selection of case studies on CSO engagement in the project cycle. It highlights innovative and successful approaches in CSO engagement from CPS through engaging CSOs in project design, implementation, and monitoring.

Country Partnership Strategy Preparation

SARD is adopting tailored approaches to enhance CSO engagement in the preparation of CPS. The project lifecycle begins with preparing the CPS. The following are examples of recent CPSs prepared with CSO inputs in South Asia and how each team customized its approach to suit local circumstances. In Nepal, after the transition to a new federal system of government, the resident mission consulted with CSOs widely to hear various perspectives, including those of the excluded and vulnerable. In Bangladesh, online consultations expanded the engagement of CSOs in CPS preparation.

Nepal CPS consultations engaged CSOs from across the country to ensure a variety of voices were heard, including those of the excluded and vulnerable. ADB approved the CPS for Nepal for 2020–2024 in September 2019. In developing the CPS, the Nepal Resident Mission (NRM) conducted extensive consultations, including with CSOs, throughout the country. The government was particularly keen to ensure that ADB conducted comprehensive consultations given the country's recent transition to a federal system. NRM staff consulted with 555 individuals from government, CSOs, the private sector, and academia across the 7 provinces. SARD was also careful to include a wide audience including both groups already aware of ADB's work and those representing excluded and vulnerable people. CSO representatives attended in high numbers and NRM staff attributed this success to not relying on email communications (many regional CSOs do not have access to email) and following up on all invitation letters by telephone. NRM staff and consultants visited each province at least a week before the consultation to remind participants of the event. NRM documented the consultations and, at the end of the process, produced a video story, and reported on all consultations, which helped inform the development of the CPS.

The Nepal Resident Mission produced a video on the consultation process for the CPS. The objective was to gather views from a range of stakeholders, including CSOs, on how ADB can be most effective in supporting Nepal's inclusive and sustainable economic development (photo by ADB's Nepal Resident Mission).

Scan to watch video

Indira Poudel
Vice President
NGO Federation, Kaski
Province 4

Through this consultation we came to know that various ADB projects have been successful in Nepal.

Online consultations in Bangladesh expanded the reach of CSO engagement in CPS preparation. The Bangladesh Resident Mission (BRM) conducted consultations for the new CPS (2021–2025) during increasing COVID-19 infection rates in March 2021. While normal participation in these consultations is usually around 50%–60%, 60 out of 69 invited groups attended, which BRM staff believe was due to the online format. Dhaka is a traffic-clogged city and in the past, BRM held consultations at its offices in Dhaka. Many participants spent several hours traveling to attend consultations. Using online communication platforms such as Zoom improved attendance. ADB should consider using this approach more often to continue high levels of CSO engagement.

Operational and advocacy organizations attended the consultation and provided feedback on the draft plan. These included the Asia Foundation, the Association of Development Agencies, BRAC, Caritas, NGO Forum on ADB, Palli Karma Sahayak Foundation (PKSF), Rangpur Dinajpur Rural Service, Save the Children, Transparency International, Water Aid, and World Vision. BRM staff said that ADB incorporated CSO inputs into the new CPS, particularly in education quality, service delivery, governance, natural resources, food and food safety mechanization, climate, gender equality and social inclusion (GESI), urban health, energy efficiency, safeguards, nature-based solutions, water and sanitation, governance, youth entrepreneurship, and skills development. The CPS includes the following statement to cement engagement with CSOs:

> **Efforts will be made to deepen the ongoing collaboration with civil society organizations for community-based approaches in urban health, water management, gender equality and social inclusion, and urban services.**[17]

TAKEAWAYS

- CPS consultation processes are more effective when aligned with local circumstances.

- ADB's resident missions in South Asia have dedicated resources on adequate preparation for CPS consultations, including resources to contact and follow up with participants.

- Consulting widely and including CSOs that represent excluded and vulnerable people ensure the CPS considers voices from all levels of society.

- Government engagement and commitment to comprehensive consultation processes boosts the potential for engagement with CSOs. This is critical for conducting robust consultations during CPS preparation.

- Online consultations can generate greater levels of participation than holding a consultation in one physical location.

---

[17] ADB. 2021. *Country Partnership Strategy: Bangladesh, 2021–2025—Sustain Growth, Build Resilience, and Foster Inclusion*. Manila.

●●●●

Project Design

Robust CSO engagement in project processing leads to improved project design. CSOs play many roles in ADB-financed operations at the project design stage. This section examines a project where advocacy CSOs engaged in project design to strengthen environmental protections in a wind power generation project in Sri Lanka led to innovative design improvements. A second example demonstrates how CSO engagement strengthened the gender elements of a project.

Advocacy CSO inputs during project design lead to stronger environmental protections. The Mannar Island Wind Power Generation Project is an example of how strong CSO engagement and a robust schedule of consultations from the SARD team led to improved project design. Mannar Island in the Northern Province of Sri Lanka is a dry and barren island subject to monsoon winds, making it well-suited to renewable energy projects. Electricity infrastructure was damaged during the domestic conflict. Enter the Government of Sri Lanka and ADB's Wind Power Generation Project, a 100-megawatt wind park project approved in 2017 with a $200 million loan to the government. Its aim is to increase access to reliable and renewable clean energy.[18] In designing the project, ADB and the government consulted with a range of CSOs. These included environmental and advocacy organizations such as the Environmental Foundation Limited, the Centre for Environmental Justice, the Young Zoologists Association, and the Ceylon Bird Club. These CSOs raised concerns about the project's impact on local birdlife. The project team met with them and listened to their concerns about the wind farm's proposed location on the Central Asian Flyway (a major bird migration path), on Mannar Island critical habitats, and the Vankalai Sanctuary, and other concerns about procedural matters related to the timing of the environmental impact assessment.

> **Engagement of CSOs in the project can be more effective if it starts at the concept stages of the projects. They may be involved right from the project design stages.**
>
> — *Respondent from survey on ADB's CSO engagement in South Asia*

The Ceylon Bird Club's annual waterbird census showed that the Vankalai Sanctuary is host to species including the Eurasian wigeon, the Indian spot-billed duck, the greater flamingo, and the black-tailed godwit. The site is 5.5 kilometers southeast of a proposed wind turbine installment. The sanctuary hosts 56,000 Eurasian wigeons in winter or 22% of the international flyway population of the species. CSOs were deeply concerned that birds using the Central Asian Flyway would be injured or killed in the moving blades of the wind turbines.

---

[18] ADB. Sri Lanka: Wind Power Generation Project.

The project team also consulted with church groups, women's rural development societies, local fishery societies, and other CBOs. Their concerns included the possible effects of turbines on fish stocks, the sound of the turbines, and whether the project area would be fenced off, which means livestock would lose access to grazing areas.

During these consultations, the advocacy group NGO Forum on ADB worked with the Ceylon Bird Club to present their concerns, which the NGO Forum outlined on its website.[19] The CSOs were concerned that the bird collision risk assessment was not conducted at the correct time of year to accurately reflect the migrating bird population and there would need to be a shutdown-on-demand option for the turbines to protect migrating birds.

As a result of these consultations, the project team made two changes to the project design. The first was reducing the number of turbines from 56 to 39 (to ensure efficient use of land resources and in response to overcoming land acquisition and land ownership issues). The second was installing a state-of-the-art radar bird detection system that tracks bird movements and temporarily shuts down the turbines if bird movement is detected. This proposal caused some concern for the Ceylon Bird Club, which they presented in their response to an ADB correspondence describing the plan to install the radar system: "Again radar monitoring of birds and turbine shutdown is described. Can this be expected ever to be done?"[20]

Advocacy CSO inputs led to improvements in the project design of a wind power generation project in Sri Lanka (photo by ADB).

The wind farm is now operational and the President of Sri Lanka opened it in December 2020. It is the largest wind farm in Sri Lanka and, besides hydro, the largest low-cost renewable energy project in the country, with a capacity of 345,600 megawatt hours per year. This is equivalent to saving about 265,700 tons of carbon dioxide emissions per year.[21]

---

19 NGO Forum on ADB. Wind Power Generation Project.
20 Footnote 19; and P. Samaraweera. 2017. Correspondence from Ceylon Bird Club to ADB. 23 October.
21 J. Kolantharaj and M. Ullrich. 2021. Scaling Up Wind Power in Sri Lanka. Development Asia. 10 June.

The project installed the radar system and deployed bird monitoring teams to determine the project's impact on birdlife. As of late 2021, the turbines have injured no birds. The bird monitoring system was not part of the earlier project design and was developed after consultations with CSOs.

CSO inputs strengthen gender dimensions of project design. Engaging with government agencies and CSOs at the onset of project preparation was a priority in developing the Strengthening Gender Inclusive Initiatives in Maldives Project.[22] The project strengthens the government's capacity to implement gender-inclusive initiatives as aligned with its existing gender equality laws and plans addressing inequalities and mitigating impacts of COVID-19 on women, including achieving SDG 5.

> **The key lesson is that involvement of the CSOs should be right from the stage of project identification and should continue over the entire life cycle of the project, including design, implementation, monitoring, operation and maintenance, and evaluation.**
>
> — *Respondent from survey on ADB's CSO engagement in South Asia*

The project outputs were designed after consultations with government agencies and CSOs at the project concept stage. An important output of the project is supporting partnerships among Maldivian CSOs, local councils, women's development committees, and the government to promote the prevention of gender-based violence and access to quality services for survivors. ADB consulted 15 CSOs during the due diligence stage. ADB will continue to consult with CSOs and seek their inputs in the final project design, including their potential engagement during implementation. During implementation, the project will support the capacity development of interested and qualified CSOs to help them prepare proposals and build a partnership with the Ministry of Gender, Family, and Social Services and local councils in implementing gender and social activities.

This case demonstrates good practice in early engagement with CSOs during the design phase. In this example, CSOs did not only suggest how the project should maximize development impact but also participated in the design process as potential delivery partners. By engaging early with CSOs, ADB can design and incorporate capacity development support to maximize the benefit from CSO engagement during project implementation.

---

[22] ADB. Maldives: Strengthening Gender Inclusive Initiatives Project. Case study text by Puri Gamon, associate social development officer (gender), ADB South Asia Department.

TAKEAWAYS

- Engaging with CSOs early in project design creates a more effective and sustainable project. Project teams need to consider how this early engagement is resourced.

- Advocacy CSOs will often engage with ADB in a voluntary capacity during project design as representatives of beneficiaries or target groups. Project teams that have remained open to this engagement have seen that it can have positive impacts on the project.

- Engaging CSOs early and often strengthens project design and allows project teams to identify CSOs that might be suitable to hire as consultants or service providers during implementation.

- By engaging CSOs early, ADB can design and incorporate capacity support programs to maximize the benefits from CSO engagement as consultants or service providers during implementation.

Project Implementation

CSOs can be engaged as service providers or consultants on ADB-financed loans or grant projects. They less frequently partner with ADB and member governments on ADB-financed operations. They may also act in a voluntary capacity to provide community services on ADB-financed loans or grant projects as opposed to working in a paid capacity. As consultants, they may provide coordination or capacity development, special initiatives to support implementation strategies or help implement safeguard and gender action plans (GAPs) or gender equality and social inclusion (GESI) action plans. As partners, they provide specialist knowledge and expertise that is difficult to find elsewhere. As volunteers, they are usually called on to act as representatives of local communities or groups of women, youth, urban poor, persons with disabilities, and private sector operators.

Coordination and Capacity Development

CSOs perform a range of roles in coordination and capacity development during project implementation in SARD. One of the most frequent ways CSOs are engaged in ADB-financed loans and grants in South Asia is through the provision of consulting services. Often, this is in the context of coordination and capacity development activities. The three examples in this section demonstrate the roles that CSOs play across two sectors (education and urban development) and highlight the approaches and strategies that succeeded. In the first example, from Bangladesh, CSOs provide niche expertise that strengthens the design of capacity development in project implementation. In this project, they act as both partners and consulting services providers. The second example, from Nepal, demonstrates that networks of grassroots CSOs are powerful instruments for coordination. The third example, from an urban water project in Sri Lanka, demonstrates how a local CSO performed essential community coordination functions and how effective project documentation of CSO engagement can improve project outcomes.

Industry associations play a multifaceted role in project implementation. The Government of Bangladesh, ADB, and other development partners established an ambitious target to train 800,000 young people in 130 occupations under the Skills for Employment Investment Program (SEIP) under a multitranche financing facility (MFF) which ADB approved in July 2014.

Under the SEIP MFF, the government partnered with industry associations to design and deliver training courses suited to industry needs. The government engaged nine industry associations as partners under Tranche 1. Working with industry associations (which are classified as CSOs)[23] and NGO training institutes, the SEIP partnered with these CSOs to impart skills training programs aligned to industry needs to young people in Bangladesh. The objective is that 60% of the trainees will find employment within 6 months of certification. NGOs, which are partner organizations of the government-established PKSF, delivered microcredit and skills training programs under the MFF. According to the SEIP website, as of 25 September 2021, 495,735 students have enrolled in technical and vocational education and training (TVET) courses, of whom 155,660 are women; 435,292 have received certificates and 316,488 are employed.

Trainer Kamali Chakma shows tools to trainees participating in the Skills for Employment Investment Program in Chittagong. The program aims to scale up qualifications to contribute to higher growth in priority sectors (photo by ADB).

---

23   The industry associations are "globally known entities unique to the six sectors and are registered as not-for-profit trade organizations under the Trade Organization Act, 1961 (amended). Their main objective is to serve the interests of their member enterprises for increased growth and competitiveness, of which human resource development is a common priority." ADB. 2016. Bangladesh. Skills for Employment Investment Program (Tranche 2) and Minor Change to the Facility.

Trainees learn dressmaking at a training center, run by Bangladesh Garment Manufacturers and Exporters Association (BGMEA), an industry association, as part of the Skills for Employment Investment Program to scale-up qualifications of the labor force to contribute in higher growth of priority sectors.

Under Tranche 2, which was approved in November 2016, the government is expanding its partnerships with industry associations to include three additional sectors: agro-processing, tourism and hospitality, and nursing and health technology. Industry associations will provide $3.5 million in cash and in-kind contributions to the project.[24] This represents the highest level of CSO engagement, i.e., partnership, with significant resources contributed by the project partners, in this case, the industry associations.

Lastly, CSOs provide guidance and oversight to the project. All industry associations are on the project steering committee, along with other CSO representatives. As one project team member said during an interview, "Industry associations know the market and industry demands much better than we do. It was not possible to deliver good training without them." The project procured each of the industry associations for this program using single-source selection (direct contracting), where only one contractor is invited to bid. Direct contracting was justified in this project in recognition of the unique role the industry associations have in advising the government on the skills required for each industry sector.

Networks of grassroots CSOs are effective mechanisms for community coordination. The Bagmati River Basin has important cultural significance for Nepal. The Bagmati River is the major river in the Kathmandu Valley, and its water is considered holy. It also provides most of Kathmandu's drinking water. Many cultural and religious ceremonies take place on its banks. Over the years, rapid urbanization and poor solid waste management turned the river into the equivalent of an open sewer with high fecal loads. In the dry season, 80% of the river flow is withdrawn for town water.

In 2013, ADB approved the Bagmati River Basin Improvement Project, which aimed to institutionalize integrated water resources management. The original project engaged CSOs for three packages: community mobilization, rainwater harvesting, and watershed management. For community mobilization, ADB engaged the Integrated Development Society Nepal (IDS), an experienced national CSO. IDS built a civil society platform, the

---

24   ADB. Bangladesh: Skills for Employment Investment Program - Tranche 2.

Bagmati Beautification Concern Platform (BBCP). The BBCP is a network of 457 small community CSOs.[25] It elected a committee and provided training in leadership, governance, GESI, gender analysis, event management, and integrated water resource management. The platform members enforced agreed practices for community waste segregation and recycling, vermicomposting, and rooftop gardening. The platform members encouraged community vigilance around solid waste dumping in the river.

When additional financing for the Bagmati River Basin Improvement Project was approved in 2019, the project team wanted to continue the strong community engagement and knew a grassroots network would be a valuable asset.[26] Familiar with IDS's work on the BBCP, the project awarded a contract to IDS in August 2020. The IDS assignment was to continue work on the NGO package for River Environment Improvement Through Community Leadership Development.

IDS is delivering the same strong community coordination and networking it provided under the original project to improve the health of other parts of the Bagmati. Also, under the additional financing for the project, IDS is continuing to work with the existing civil society platform, which covers Sundarijal to Sinamangal. IDS also works on other stretches and tributaries in the lower basin (Sinamangal to Balkhu) to form and link new civil society platforms into a federation of civil society platforms. They also continue promoting waste segregation, composting, and recycling. IDS works with local schools to raise awareness of solid waste management best practices and with *guthis* (local social organizations) to develop heritage management plans for the maintenance and restoration of heritage buildings to be restored along the river. IDS has produced successful communications campaigns and tutorial videos as part of the project, with one video receiving over 14,000 views from local people through these extensive networks. They also produced two documentaries on the project.

The success of the Bagmati River Basin Improvement Project depends on the active participation of communities and civil society organizations in conserving and managing basin water resources.

25   The platform was registered as an NGO, thereby giving it a legal status.
26   ADB. Nepal: Bagmati River Basin Improvement Project – Additional Financing.

IDS reported that high volunteerism is a key driver behind BBCP. The community was initially skeptical of IDS activities but eventually IDS successfully engaged them in leading river health monitoring. IDS also reported that the platform has good prospects for sustainability. The BBCP is undertaking various small-scale social enterprises and is still going strong on its own merits. IDS suggested that volunteerism in the lower basin under the current project will be more challenging as the more urbanized areas of Kathmandu have less of a volunteer ethos. IDS work on this project demonstrates that gaining community trust and having community credibility are important elements for working successfully with grassroots networks, which often comprise mostly volunteers.

Recurring collaboration enhances local CSO capacity to perform essential community coordination roles. In 1989, a group of human settlement activists established the Sevanatha Urban Resource Center in Colombo to improve shelter and livelihood options for urban poor people.[27] Sevanatha has been involved in this sector ever since and has a high level of expertise in this area of work. In 2013, ADB hired Sevanatha Urban Resource Center under the Greater Colombo Wastewater Management Project and Sevanatha successfully delivered community coordination activities. The outcome of this work was the construction of a small sewerage network, treatment, and disposal setup in an underserved settlement in Colombo. The construction was carried out by the beneficiary community through their community-based organization. The CSO managed the overall construction activities.

> ❝ **Engaging with CSOs as contractors has a very positive impact on community awareness generation, participation, and inclusion.**
>
> — *Respondent from survey on ADB's CSO engagement in South Asia*

In 2012, ADB approved the MFF Greater Colombo Water and Wastewater Management Improvement Investment Program with the overall objective of improving water supply and wastewater service and management in Greater Colombo.[28] The CSO reported that its first assignment under Tranche 1 allowed them to develop capacity to engage with implementing agencies, to implement a project involving construction and procurement of materials and labor, and to become more accustomed to ADB's financial reporting requirements. From the government and ADB sides, the CSO's experience in managing social issues and community mobilizing helped them resolve several matters of concern.

Under Tranche 3, approved in 2015, the Sevanatha Urban Resource Center was recruited to (i) carry out a socioeconomic analysis, GESI activities, and assessment of wastewater service delivery; (ii) facilitate the project management unit (PMU) and the design, supervision, and institutional development consultants in management of resettlement and post resettlement

---

[27] Sevanatha Urban Resource Centre. About Sevanatha Urban Resource Centre.
[28] ADB. Sri Lanka: Greater Colombo Water and Wastewater Management Improvement Investment Program (Facility Concept).

program; (iii) lead community awareness and people's participation; and (iv) implement citizen education for wastewater service management, and health and hygiene education.[29] Sevanatha Urban Resource Center is building on the work it did under earlier tranches. One success factor in Sevanatha's engagement is how SARD built Sevanatha's capacity over many years to engage with ADB and the partner government on projects of this nature.

Another success case of Tranche 3 was the consultation and participation plan. The plan outlines the role of civil society and the contracted NGO, and includes targets for participation, the type of participation envisaged, the objectives, who is responsible, the time frame, and the respective budget for each line item. Having this level of explicit detail in the project planning documents plays a major role in ensuring that activities unfold as planned. This level of planning is rarely detailed in ADB project documents and thus an area for SARD to consider for improving engagement (Table 2). Participation plans (also called consultation and participation plans) are required if the summary poverty reduction and social strategy (a mandatory annexure to the report and recommendation of the President) indicates that the project has planned meaningful CSO engagement.[30] In this case, a participation plan is mandatory and should be linked to relevant project documents and resources identified to help ensure the planned participation of CSOs is delivered. A CSO participation plan may be embedded within the GAP, GESI action plan or safeguards documents only if all planned CSO engagement is already documented there. SARD, and all ADB regional departments, should observe this requirement. Consultation and participation plans address the objectives of the CSO engagement, types of participation, timeframes, budget, and responsibility for engagement.

Table 2: Snapshot of the Consultation and Participation Plan for the Greater Colombo Water and Wastewater Management Improvement Investment Program Tranche 3

C&P Activity	Target Stakeholders	Type of Participation	Objectives of the C&P Activity	Responsible Unit/Persons	Time Frame	Cost Estimate
1 consultation workshop with underserved settlements communities (end users and affected persons) from the project area (half day)	Representatives of under served settlements	Information sharing Consultation	Introduce the project, highlighting its importance and benefits Discuss importance of participation in waste water management groups in underserved and unserved areas, maintenance of facilities, opportunities for participation in project Mitigate potential conflict	PMU, DSIDC, in cooperation with project NGO, and contractors	Year 1	Consultation workshop = $750

C&P = consultation and participation, DSIDC = design, supervision, and institutional development consultants, NGO = nongovernment organization, PMU = project management unit.
Source: ADB. 2015. Greater Colombo Water and Wastewater Management Improvement Investment Program – Tranche 3. Periodic Financing Request Report.

---

[29] ADB. 2015. Greater Colombo Water and Wastewater Management Improvement Investment Program – Tranche 3. Periodic Financing Request Report.
[30] Refer to Appendix 1 for the definition of "planned meaningful CSO engagement."

TAKEAWAYS

- Private sector representative organizations, which many people do not realize are CSOs, are excellent partners on some ADB-financed projects, particularly in education. They can contribute significant expertise and cofinancing.

- One example of niche expertise that CSOs provide is strengthening the design of capacity development activities in project implementation.

- Networks of grassroots CSOs are powerful instruments for wide-scale community coordination activities and can work with communities to generate high levels of community ownership and sustainable project interventions, thus increasing impact.

- Grassroots CSOs require support (capacity development, materials and other resources, funding) to be effective implementation partners in ADB-financed projects.

- Local CSOs bring value in community coordination where they can bring or gain trust and local understanding to a project.

- Repeat engagement of CSOs provides ADB with the opportunity to build an organization's capacity to work with ADB and government processes.

- Single-source selection, or direct contracting, may facilitate procurement when engaging a CSO with a niche or specialized skill set.

- Detailed project documentation of the roles of CSOs, particularly in their terms of reference and in consultation and participation plans, facilitates smooth implementation.

- Project teams need to orient CSOs to ADB processes early, particularly at procurement.

Special Initiatives during Project Implementation

CSOs offer innovative strategies and approaches that strengthen project implementation. CSOs play a number of special roles that strengthen project implementation. In this section, projects from India, the Maldives, and Sri Lanka demonstrate the roles that CSOs play in SARD projects to strengthen project implementation. In the first example, CSOs act as a bridge among project stakeholders to deliver innovative outcomes on a water project. In the second example, CSOs will bring tailored community behavior change approaches to an urban waste project. In the final example, an international CSO worked closely with private sector stakeholders to optimize project impact.

CSOs act as a bridge among project stakeholders to deliver innovative outcomes. In three districts of West Bengal, over 15 million people live with substandard groundwater quality. Drinking water in these three districts is contaminated with chemicals, including arsenic and fluoride. Groundwater salinity is also an issue. Approved in 2018, the ADB-financed West Bengal Drinking Water Sector Improvement Project aims to provide 24/7 continuous household rural water supply to 2.6 million people using a smart water management system across 66 *gram panchayats* (governing bodies at the village level). The West Bengal Drinking Water Sector Improvement Project is partnering with the Japan Fund for Prosperous and Resilient Asia and the Pacific (JFPR), the Urban Climate Change Resilience Trust Fund, and the World Health Organization. [31]

The project recognizes the need for widespread, continuous, and meaningful participation of stakeholders focusing on poor and vulnerable groups. The project contracted two NGOs to undertake this work, Sigma Foundation and Taru-Ramakrishna Mission East Medinipur (a consortium). The Sigma Foundation is a research and advocacy NGO with a strong grassroots base in the community. The Ramakrishna Mission also has a strong base in the community and has been working with local people for decades and has a high level of credibility and strong community support.

An important impact of engaging Sigma and Ramakrishna Mission is the role they play as a bridge between project stakeholders. Each NGO covers one project district and actioned initiatives to strengthen project implementation. In each project area, working closely with government agencies and the project implementation unit, they take on many roles, including implementing safeguard plans and completing household surveys on water supply. They raise community awareness and implement components of the GESI action plan, including school outreach. The project team described this as their "root-level" work, i.e., the core activities they are contracted to do.

However, the work they do extends beyond those tasks. The NGOs act as a bridge not only between the community and the project team but also among all project stakeholders. According to the ADB project team, the project implementation unit, the Public Health Engineering Department (PHED), the contractors, the smart water management consultant, and the design and supervision engineers all work with the NGOs. It is a complicated network of organizations, but the project involves the NGOs in each aspect to some degree, including the more technical engineering components. "The NGOs are very important stakeholders in this project," said one team member. The NGOs' engagement in multiple aspects of the project, and their key facilitation roles, attest to their importance during project implementation.

These NGOs undertake other work that directly strengthens implementation strategies, such as working with the *gram panchayats* and the implementing agency and the PHED on an agreement for managing water supply to rural areas and 80 of the state's 114 municipalities. The project's sustainability rests on a new agreement as to who will operate and maintain the system between the *gram panchayats* and the state government PHED. The NGOs helped draft this model memorandum of understanding, playing a vital facilitation role

---

[31]   ADB. India: West Bengal Drinking Water Sector Improvement Project.

between the *gram panchayats* and the state government. They also work with the PHED and local communities in identifying locations for water management centers, which will house smart water supply assets and equipment in each project area. These NGOs play a central role in ensuring the project succeeds and is sustainable.

Another special strategy used to strengthen project implementation is developing model water and sanitation safety plans. ADB arranged for the Centre for Science and Environment, a CSO in New Delhi, to deliver a training session for the two project NGOs on how to prepare a water and sanitation safety plan. Both NGOs have now prepared plans. This is a novel approach and ADB hopes the government will use this strategy for developing water and sanitation safety plans across the state, not just in the 66 *gram panchayats* for this project. Sigma Foundation received the Water Champions 2021 Award from the Centre for Science and Environment for developing their model plan.[32]

CSOs apply tailored community behavior change approaches. With growing tourism and urbanization, the Maldives faces the challenge of what to do with over 774 tons per day of mixed solid waste brought to the regional waste management facility in Thilafushi. The Greater Malé Environmental Improvement and Waste Management Project provides a sustainable solution with a modern waste collection, sorting, transfer, treatment, and disposal system.[33] The project uses a 3R (reduce, reuse, recycle) community awareness and behavior change strategy. The project will finance enhanced community-based island waste management systems on 32 inhabited outer islands and will benefit 216,000 people, roughly half the population of the Maldives.[34]

Educating and changing the behavior of people in a large project catchment area requires the expertise of a CSO. The government will recruit a CSO under an attached JFPR grant to deliver strategies to support project implementation and deliver the behavior change campaign.

The CSO will design and deliver a tailored public awareness and community capacity building campaign, working with local CSOs and other stakeholders, using social and traditional media, to motivate sustainable behavior change for solid waste management in local communities. It will also support the government with GAP implementation.

For the community awareness component, the CSO will develop a public awareness and communications strategy and plan. The communications strategy will include activities to inform and guide behavior change interventions. One of the targets is to provide support to the communities to institutionalize the change. The communications strategy will also guide the development of a project website and the setting up of social media accounts (Facebook, Twitter, Instagram, and YouTube). Social media and Viber groups are well-used so messages can be easily passed on and these platforms work well in the Maldives.

32 Sigma Foundation. SIGMA Foundation bags the Water Champions 2021 Award by CSE, New Delhi.
33 ADB. Maldives: Greater Malé Environmental Improvement and Waste Management Project.
34 ADB. 2018. ADB Assistance to Improve Environmental Protection in Maldives. News Release. 29 June.

CSOs work closely with private sector stakeholders to optimize project impact. The Skills Sector Enhancement Program approved in 2014 is a results-based loan improving the employability of the Sri Lankan workforce, particularly young people. The project focuses on four sectors: building and construction, light manufacturing and engineering, information technology, and tourism and hospitality. The project is working with industry sector skills councils (ISSCs), which are CSOs representing the private sector.[35] The partnership between the ISSCs and the government is formalized in a memorandum of understanding.

> **Orient the NGOs, give very clear guidance on how an ADB project should operate. It is important to orient the NGO partner before applying and after onboarding to avoid any misunderstanding.**
>
> — *Interviewee for ADB's report on CSO engagement in South Asia, 2015-2021*

The additional financing for the Skills Sector Enhancement Program, with an attached JFPR grant, was approved in 2018 and set additional GESI targets for TVET participation.[36] The project team determined that strengthening private sector engagement in TVET delivery and supporting women's employment in unconventional areas were tasks that could be best performed by an international NGO and conducted a roadshow to talk to NGOs with expertise in TVET and gender in Sri Lanka. When the project advertised the consultancy in 2018, the team contacted multiple NGOs to inform them of the opportunity. Unlike most commercial consulting firms, many of these NGOs were not registered in ADB's Consultant Management System (CMS). The project team shared information on how these NGOs should register in CMS to submit expressions of interest. This initial support to orient them to ADB and government processes was a necessary step. As a result, six international NGOs registered in the CMS for the first time and most of these submitted expressions of interest.

The project awarded the contract to Plan Australia, the grant implementation firm, under the attached JFPR-funded grant on Demonstrating Innovative Approaches for Private Sector and Women's Empowerment in Technical Vocation Education and Training in Sri Lanka.[37] Oxfam in Sri Lanka is now leading this work after the Plan Australia Sri Lanka Office closed down in 2020.[38]

---

[35] ADB. 2021. Sri Lanka: Skills Sector Enhancement Program (Additional Financing). Updated Program Implementation Document.

[36] ADB. Sri Lanka: Skills Sector Enhancement Program - Additional Financing.

[37] ADB. 2018. Sri Lanka: Skills Sector Enhancement Program (Additional Financing): Japan Fund for Poverty Reduction Grant - Demonstrating Innovative Approaches for Private Sector and Women's Empowerment in TVET in Sri Lanka.

[38] It was understood that Plan Australia had envisioned working with Plan Sri Lanka on this contract but Plan withdrew from the country in late 2019. Oxfam Sri Lanka is now leading this work under a subcontract from Plan Australia signed in May 2020.

Oxfam brings its expertise in engaging with and linking private sector representative organizations and community-based organizations to maximize the project's impact. Oxfam's role is supporting the ISSCs in activities and subprojects that increase the employability of young women, offer entrepreneurship development programs with a focus on young women, and help industry sectors apply gender-inclusive recruitment practices. For the tourism ISSC, this includes working with local homestay associations, which are private sector-oriented CSOs. Oxfam helped the ISSCs convene a women's advisory council to increase their sensitivity to women's issues. The new women's advisory council includes women representing larger multinational and national companies and successful women business leaders and includes 19 members with representatives from three regional chambers of commerce (also classified as CSOs). The women's advisory council helps the ISSCs sharpen their gender focus and plans, provide technical support to industry planning on gender initiatives, and supports industry and networking events. For example, a businesswoman from the women's advisory council offered seminars for 300–400 women on issues in the TVET sector. Oxfam sees the involvement and commitment of these high-level businesswomen as a unique and innovative aspect of the program.

TAKEAWAYS

- CSOs offer innovative and tailored strategies and approaches that strengthen the implementation of ADB-financed projects in South Asia.

- CSOs can work effectively on private sector-focused projects to increase project impact.

- Engaging CSOs in all aspects of the project (including the technical side) increases their engagement and ability to provide specialist services and offer innovative solutions.

- Clear documentation on the roles for CSOs on ADB projects helps all parties maximize the added value CSOs bring and reduces misunderstandings.

- Orienting CSOs to ADB and government process early in the engagement assists with smooth project implementation.

- Scoping CSOs and their capacities to deliver during project design helps achieve maximum benefit from CSO engagement.

- ADB's CMS is challenging for CSOs to navigate and they need support.

Delivery of Social Services

CSOs are active in social service delivery during the implementation of ADB projects in South Asia. Three projects in this section highlight how the niche expertise that CSOs offer is highly effective for social service delivery. The first case describes the valuable services an organization for persons with disabilities delivered in a voluntary capacity to an ADB-financed education project in Bhutan. The second project examines the work of several NGOs delivering social services to increase resilience under a community flood management and river erosion prevention project in India. The third project looks at how microfinance CSOs provided a novel and sustainable financing model for livelihood restoration in an emergency in Nepal. Beyond the three case studies presented, CSOs deliver social services in other sectors including health, energy, urban development, and agriculture and food security. ADB's *A Sourcebook for Engaging with Civil Society Organizations in Asian Development Bank Operations* provides more information, including a box on grassroots CSO assistance with the pandemic response in Sri Lanka, Nepal, and India.[39]

Disabled people's organization provides specialized advice in increasing inclusion on an education project. To meet the economic needs for competitiveness and sustained growth in Bhutan, the Skills Training and Education Pathways Upgradation Project supports the government in expanding and upgrading the TVET system for modern, diversified, and job-oriented skills development.[40] Under this project, the Ministry of Labor and Human Resources (MOLHR) partners with private technical training institutes to deliver critical skills training programs. Aside from ensuring that 30% of trainers trained are women, the project also targets intervention for persons with disabilities (PWDs) so that 5% of the total student beneficiaries can be PWDs

However, in the first 2 years of implementation, no PWD applied to join the program. MOLHR financed private training providers to deliver training programs specifically for PWDs, but the lack of experience and required facilities of the private institutes in running such a specialized inclusive program posed another challenge. At that point, MOLHR (the executing agency), reached out to the Disabled People's Organization of Bhutan (DPOB) for assistance to advise the private training institutes on how to conduct inclusive training programs dedicated for PWDs.

The DPOB is based in Thimphu, operates nationwide, and has been registered with the Civil Society Organizations Authority since 2010. Its mission is to promote the physical, psychological, and socioeconomic well-being of PWDs through a rights-based approach. The DPOB is a cross-disability representative organization providing policy advice and representation to government and organizations on subjects that affect the lives of PWDs. On this project, DPOB is helping ensure that training institutes are providing training appropriately and ensuring inclusive services such as accommodation, transport, and logistics are available for students with disabilities. Since not all facilities are designed for PWDs, the ministry supports private training providers to provide inclusive training programs responding to the needs of PWDs with guidance from the DPOB.

---

[39] ADB. 2021. *A Sourcebook for Engaging with Civil Society Organizations in Asian Development Bank Operations*. Manila. Box 14.

[40] ADB. Bhutan: Skills Training and Education Pathways Upgradation Project.

Few programs target PWDs in Bhutan. Thus, a targeted TVET program intervention is a major contribution toward a more inclusive society. Private training institutes deliver the training with technical support and expert guidance from the DPOB. This collaboration among the government, private sector, and the DPOB ensures that students with disabilities receive much-needed skills for employment. From 27 May to 26 October 2021, the project supported 45 PWDs to undertake specialized training programs on tailoring, bakery, spa, and massage. The DPOB helps MOLHR add an important socially inclusive dimension to the project on a purely voluntary basis. The ministry plans to organize another training in collaboration with the DPOB.

NGOs deliver social services to increase resilience under a community flood management and river erosion prevention project. The Brahmaputra River in India is the world's fourth-largest river. Since the Great Assam Earthquake in 1950, the river has widened significantly. Regional development is hindered by frequent flooding and riverbank erosion. The Assam Integrated Flood and Riverbank Erosion Risk Management Investment Program aims to promote people's livelihoods through comprehensive flood and riverbank erosion management measures, which will provide protection from river erosion and floods with a focus on the most vital areas of economic and national interest.[41] The Assam Integrated Flood and Riverbank Erosion Risk Management Investment Program Tranche 2 builds on the work of Tranche 1.[42]

The Assam Integrated Flood and Riverbank Erosion Risk Management Investment Program is helping raise the riverbanks of the Brahmaputra. Nongovernment organizations deliver social services as part of the program (photo by ADB).

To make the needed improvements to the river, the project had to resettle people and the project team felt that a local CSO, one the community trusted, would be best placed to deliver the social services needed during the resettlement. The project engaged community-based flood risk management and livelihood NGOs to support plans for resettlement through

---

41   ADB. India: Assam Integrated Flood and Riverbank Erosion Risk Management Investment Program.
42   ADB. India: Assam Integrated Flood and Riverbank Erosion Risk Management Investment Program
      Tranche 2.

participatory development of community-based flood risk management action plans and livelihoods training. The implementing agency hired two local CSOs, Scorpion and Socio-Educational Welfare Association.

The two CSOs delivered a number of social services under the project, including mobilizing volunteers to produce facemasks, animal husbandry training for project-affected people, providing free medical health check-ups for flood-affected communities and vulnerable people, and awareness-raising on sexually transmitted infections including HIV.[43]

The CSOs expressed concerns about their ability to deliver services flexibly under a hybrid time- and output-based contract. Like many CSOs, they preferred an output-based contract. They requested an output-based contract to provide the flexibility they needed to deliver the outputs the way they wanted to work. The government listened to their concerns and processed a variation of a hybrid contract to an output-based contract.

Microfinance CSOs provided a novel and sustainable financing model for livelihood restoration in an emergency. The 25 April 2015 earthquake in Nepal devastated local communities, with 31 out of Nepal's 75 districts reporting damage. Nepal's economic growth fell from 5.1% in 2014 to 3.0% in 2015 due to infrastructure damage and production disruption.[44] For rural households, the impact was not only on housing, which was considerable, but also on farmland and livestock. This directly affected the livelihoods and earning capacity of villagers.

ADB supported microcredit loans through smallholder farmer agricultural cooperatives in response to Nepal's 2015 earthquake (photo by ADB).

43   ADB. 2021. *Assam Integrated Flood and Riverbank Erosion Risk Management Investment Program - Project 2: Social Monitoring Report July-December 2020*. Manila; ADB. 2021 *Assam Integrated Flood and Riverbank Erosion Risk Management Investment Program - Project 2: Social Monitoring Report January-June 2020*. Manila.
44   ADB. 2019. *Microfinance for Disaster Recovery: Lessons from the 2015 Nepal Earthquake*. Manila.

ADB wanted to deliver sustainable support to communities in the aftermath of the emergency. ADB approved the JFPR-funded grant for the Disaster Risk Reduction and Livelihood Restoration for Earthquake-Affected Communities project on 3 September 2015.[45] The project improved livelihoods and schooling in poor and severely earthquake-affected communities, coupling construction with disaster preparedness and resilience interventions. The project rebuilt eight model schools in earthquake-affected districts to be more disaster-resilient. A second component of the project restored livelihoods through microcredit facilities. The project channeled funds through smallholder farmer agricultural cooperatives (SFACs) in the three earthquake-affected districts of Dhading, Nuwakot, and Rasuwa.

ADB and the government work with SFACs on other projects and they were proven partners for the implementation of livelihood restoration activities through microcredit services. The Small Farmers Development Bank provided loans to the SFACs in three districts, who then provided loans to their members for livelihood restoration activities. The loans provided quick financial assistance so beneficiaries could invest in income generation activities, particularly microenterprises, and in livestock and agriculture to revive their livelihoods.

A project evaluation found that the net income of beneficiaries of the microcredit program was much higher than that of nonbeneficiaries. Net revenue from the income-generating activities for March 2017 to February 2018 was NRs84,000 ($701) for beneficiaries and NRs39,000 ($325) for nonbeneficiaries. The income discrepancy between the two groups can be attributed to the beneficiary group's larger investment resources, including loans from SFACs. Also, beneficiaries used more resources than the nonbeneficiaries to invest in fixed assets, such as equipment and machinery, which may have contributed to lower operating expenses and higher productivity (footnote 44). As one project team member said, "The beauty of microfinance is that the beneficiaries can get a loan, and then get another loan, and there is ongoing access to financing. Microfinance allows people to borrow for feed, crops, and other goods and services to continue their livelihood activities. In emergencies, an established relationship with microfinance institutions (MFIs) is essential to quickly and smoothly deliver financial services to affected households."

The project showed that microcredit as a disaster response can be an innovative and effective option if there is an existing relationship with microcredit providers. Microfinance can yield greater long-term benefits than short-term emergency assistance grants. When SFACs or nongovernment organization microfinance institutions (NGO-MFIs) and their borrowers have established a relationship of trust, they become an efficient and smooth mechanism for delivering financial services to disaster-affected households.

---

[45] ADB. Nepal: Disaster Risk Reduction and Livelihood Restoration for Earthquake-Affected Communities.

TAKEAWAYS

- CSOs provide a number of social services to ADB-financed projects in South Asia.
- Close links to communities make CSOs excellent partners for community-based social service delivery.
- Specialist CSOs can offer expertise the private sector does not have.
- CSOs deliver services in a paid or voluntary capacity on ADB-financed projects in South Asia.
- Microfinance provides an innovative form of CSO social service delivery in South Asia, providing quick support for livelihood restoration. However, relationships must be mature for this to be effective.
- CSOs prefer output-based contracts as they find these better suited to the way they work.
- Some CSOs require capacity development support.

Support to Safeguards, Gender Action Plan, and Gender Equality and Social Inclusion Action Plan Implementation

Many CSOs are uniquely placed to assist in delivering social safeguard plan implementation because of their strong community relations and their understanding of local norms and community presence. CSOs support gender action plans (GAP) and gender equality and social inclusion (GESI) action plan implementation. The desk review of CSO engagement in sovereign projects in South Asia 2015–2021, found many projects planned to engage CSOs to implement safeguards, GAPs, and GESI action plans. Based on interviews with ADB staff, this engagement appears to be conventional in approach. Some project teams said they often rely on the same organizations undertaking the same type of work and there is a need for new entrants. However, some project teams said that having the same organizations engaged more than once is beneficial because they know ADB and government systems and processes.

Some CSOs are highly qualified to help support social safeguard plans because of their existing community engagement, local presence, and experience in gender and safeguards. The Climate Adaptation in Vennar Subbasin in Cauvery River Delta Project improves irrigation and water management in six channels covering a total command area of 78,000 hectares in the Vennar subbasin of the Cauvery delta in Tamil Nadu, India.[46]

---

46   ADB. India: Climate Adaptation in Vennar Subbasin in Cauvery Delta Project.

The project, approved in 2016, aims to strengthen the embankments of these six channels to make them more flood-resilient and enable the subbasin to better serve local people's water needs. The construction work displaced over 1,800 households. The project hired the NGO Health and Agriculture and Village Education Network (HEAVEN) to help the PMU implement the resettlement plans.

> **The executing agency engineers know how to construct canals, but CSOs are vital and crucial for social issues and working with people. This aspect is very difficult for engineers to execute. CSOs play a vital role.**
>
> — *Interviewee for ADB's report on CSO engagement in South Asia 2015-2021*

The project team reported that HEAVEN plays a critical role in community engagement. HEAVEN staff speak the local language and have the project-affected people's trust in handling the very personal task of resettlement. They recognize that each individual's case is different. HEAVEN works with each family and group to ensure the relocation process involves the least disruption and considers the affected family's needs. The project team recognizes that resettlement was one of the major tasks of this project and that HEAVEN has contributed positively to achieving the overall development impacts of the project.

In a similar vein, the implementing agency for the Uttar Pradesh Major District Roads Improvement Project hired a local NGO, Manavadhikar Samajik Manch (the Human Rights, Social and Administration Platform [MASM]), using the least-cost selection consultant recruitment method to implement the resettlement plan.[47] Approved in 2016, the project has upgraded 425 kilometers of major district roads in the State of Uttar Pradesh in India. MASM actively supported the implementing agency with seven resettlement plans, including the assessment of compensation for affected people and conducting other social activities such as on sexually transmitted infections including HIV, human trafficking, and road safety awareness initiatives. MASM engaged over 900 households through outreach and 56 affected households through skills training.

> ❝ **Quality- and cost-based selection should be preferred over the least-cost selection method for service provider engagement.**
>
> — *Respondent from survey on ADB's CSO engagement in South Asia*

The project team was of the view that if the implementing agency had used another selection method (e.g., quality- and cost-based selection), then it could have ensured the continuity of CSO project staff and helped achieve outputs sooner.

CSOs are uniquely placed to work with the private sector to support GESI action plan implementation. The Disaster Resilience of Schools Project in Nepal enhances disaster risk management for human resources development as envisioned in the Post Disaster Recovery Framework and School Sector Development Plan of the Government of Nepal (post-2015 Nepal earthquake).[48] The project aims to increase the number of disaster-resilient schools and communities and improve the learning environment in schools. Heavily damaged schools will be renovated and unsafe schools retrofitted to reduce risks. Simultaneously, institutional capacity for disaster resilience will be strengthened.

ADB and the government needed an organization to help implement sensitive GESI action plan features and work with the community on more traditional skills training and infrastructure work. A consortium, including private sector engineering firms and an NGO, implemented Output 3 of the project in cooperation with the school management committees. Including a CSO in the consortium provided the crucial support to deliver the GESI action plan aspects of the school retrofits and construction. The project engaged the Rural Education and Environment Development Centre Nepal NGO to lead the school disaster risk management packages with Infrastructure Engineering Research and Consult, ECoCoDE Nepal, and Strength, which are joint venture engineering consulting firms. The NGO trains people in the community on skills relevant to the infrastructure work such as mason's training and on-the-job training for women and men.

Rural Education and Environment Development Centre Nepal ensures the requirements in the GESI action plan are incorporated in the retrofitting and construction of schools. GESI action plan features include sex-segregated toilets with improved menstrual hygiene facilities, a special needs toilet, changing rooms with a sink in the girls' toilets, and incinerators for sanitary pad disposal. The consortium also conducts sensitive training on menstrual health for girls in grades 6–12.

---

48 ADB. Nepal: Disaster Resilience of Schools Project.

BOX

Procurement Challenges in Civil Society Organizations in ADB-Financed Projects

Quotes from ADB staff interviewed and surveyed as part of this report.

"We need to rethink the procedural system for engaging CSOs."

— *Interviewee*

"For smaller NGOs, recruitment has been a nightmare."

— *Interviewee*

"Currently [there is] no distinction between NGOs and other consultants. Have a separate set of (easier) guidelines for better recognizing CSOs as distinct entities."

— *Interviewee*

Staff highlighted the following areas of concern in procurement and contracting CSOs, in both interviews and the survey:

- Due diligence issues, including difficulties with due diligence and risk assessment in the context of engaging with CSOs and identifying CSOs relevant to country operations. This topic is addressed in ADB's *A Sourcebook for Engaging with Civil Society Organizations in Asian Development Bank Operations*.[a]
- Registration in ADB's CMS is a barrier to some CSOs engaging with ADB. ADB staff report having to help CSOs with the process.
- On registering, some CSOs find ADB's CMS hard to navigate and use, particularly smaller CSOs.
- CSOs are often not familiar with ADB and government procurement and contracting processes, thus slowing down CSO recruitment and onboarding.
- Recruitment issues, including the least-cost selection recruitment method, which prioritizes the lowest bids, may result in under-resourcing for CSO components.
- Contracts, including CSOs reportedly not appreciating contract terms and a tendency toward input-based or time-based contracts, while CSOs generally prefer output-based contracts.
- Terms of reference issues, including lack of clarity about the exact terms of reference of CSO work, or CSOs not fully appreciating the scope of the terms of reference for which they applied.
- A lack of CSO understanding of ADB and government processes for submitting claims and timesheets.

Some staff indicated that a new or simplified system of procurement, tailored specifically to the needs of CSOs, is the answer. Others indicated that better orientation of CSOs to ADB and government processes early in the project cycle is required, at least at the point of procurement, and handholding throughout the procurement and contracting process. These challenges are discussed in Section 6 on Lessons and Recommendations.

ADB = Asian Development Bank, CMS = consultant management system, CSO = civil society organization.
[a] ADB. 2021. *A Sourcebook for Engaging with Civil Society Organizations in Asian Development Bank Operations*. Manila.
Source: Asian Development Bank.

TAKEAWAYS

- CSOs help governments implement safeguards, GAPs, and GESI action plans of ADB-financed loans and grants in South Asia.

- Successful implementation of safeguards, GAPs, and GESI action plans are critical to project success.

- This complex work has a human element for which CSOs are particularly well-suited due to their often long-standing engagement with and understanding of communities.

- CSOs require time to build community goodwill and trust in the absence of a long-standing engagement with communities.

- The selection method for recruitment influences the way CSOs frame their bids.

- The budget for the CSO component must be appropriate for the CSO to effectively execute these activities as CSOs do not have non-project funds.

- CSOs can be part of a private sector-led consortium.

- Least-cost selection procurement may lead to underfunded contracts for the delivery of safeguards, GAPs, and GESI action plans.

- As governments and CSOs get to know each other throughout project implementation, trust and positive engagement increases.

Target Groups and Beneficiaries

SARD involves CSOs as target groups or beneficiaries, which can increase the sustainability of a project and lead to better development outcomes. CSOs may be target groups for loan and grant projects as well as direct or indirect beneficiaries. This section highlights case studies illustrating these roles. The first case is from Bangladesh and showcases CSOs as target groups in the agriculture and natural resources sector and demonstrates how working with CBOs is ensuring sustainable and effective management of water resources. Two other projects (one from Bangladesh and one from Sri Lanka) look at CSOs as beneficiaries of microenterprise loans and microfinance.

Working with CBOs and using participatory approaches in water projects supports long-term sustainable and effective water management. In Bangladesh, over 80% of poor people live in rural areas and depend on agriculture and fishing for food and livelihoods. Effective water resource management is vital to their survival. However, the chronic deterioration of flood control, drainage, and irrigation infrastructure hamper effective water resources management. ADB and the Government of Bangladesh are committed to long-term participatory water management and recognize that community participation in designing, operating, and monitoring water infrastructure enhances performance. The additional financing for the Southwest Area Integrated Water Resources Planning and Management Project aims to enhance beneficiary participation in water resources management, particularly in the design of appropriate water resource management interventions.[49] One project output is strengthening the participatory water management organization's capacity for sustainable water resources planning and management in subproject areas.

Under the additional financing, project beneficiaries and their water management associations have developed 23 participatory subunit water management plans using a demand-driven approach. Project staff facilitated the formation of 369 water management groups (WMGs) in the project areas (267 under the additional financing), with 87,457 members, of whom 43,136 are women. These water management associations and WMGs (CSOs and CBOs) will take responsibility for operation and maintenance and help ensure sustainability.

Because of the central role WMGs play in water management planning and design, they must assume a high level of ownership in finding solutions to problems. The Bangladesh Water Development Board follows a bottom-up approach and once plans are agreed upon, they engage contractors for the construction. The WMGs also monitor the contractors' work in the field and manage minor operation and maintenance. The WMGs ensure a high level of ownership under this model as the assets will eventually be transferred to them.

Additional financing for the Southwest Area Integrated Water Resources Planning and Management Project establishes water management organizations to help select and design water use interventions in Bangladesh (photo by ADB).

49 ADB. Bangladesh: Southwest Area Integrated Water Resources Planning and Management Project Additional Financing.

Because WMG members are from the community, they are uniquely placed to resolve conflicts around water issues. Sometimes there are conflicting demands for water between farmers and fishers. WMGs work with the community to resolve these conflicts and decide on water allocation in a way that government agencies cannot.

Working with CSO MFIs enhances community access to enterprise financing, training, and marketing support. In Bangladesh, the Microenterprise Development Project promotes microenterprise development for inclusive economic growth and poverty reduction.[50] Based on the successes of the Grameen Bank in the 1980s, the Government of Bangladesh established the Palli Karma Sahayak Foundation (PKSF) in 1990 to provide wholesale funds for microfinance programs to NGO-MFIs. The project aims to improve microenterprise access to finance through the PKSF, whose partner organizations are NGO-MFIs.

Working with NGO-MFIs is rapidly expanding the number of borrowers gaining access to finance. ADB provided a loan to PKSF for $50 million under the Microenterprise Development Project in 2019 that helped 40,000 microenterprises with an average loan size of around $1,500. Because of the COVID-19 lockdown in 2020, sales of microenterprise products declined and this increased the demand for additional loans among microenterprise owners. This required PKSF to borrow an additional $50 million from ADB in December 2020 to almost double the number of borrowers who accessed microenterprise lending under the original loan to cover an additional 30,000 borrowers from partner organizations, of whom 70% are women affected by COVID-19. An ongoing technical assistance (TA) will support project implementation. PKSF disbursed the second $50 million to 98 partner organizations in August 2021.

The project ensures that lending is gender-sensitive. Through PKSF, the project will enhance partner organizational capacity in microenterprise lending by implementing improved gender-inclusive finance guidelines. Training has started for 120 partner organizations using the microenterprise finance operational guidelines.

The project is helping women access microenterprise finance through mobile-friendly applications. Three partner organizations implemented a mobile-based microenterprise financing application for 30,043 microenterprise borrowers (70% are women). Plans include PKSF's acquisition of a mobile financial service license to offer the same service at a much lower price.

Finally, the project is helping microenterprises increase sales. The project is addressing market-related challenges for selling microenterprise products (e.g., organic vegetables, dried fish, shoemaking, fish fry for hatcheries) through cluster platforms. Working with partner organizations, clusters seek to improve branding and packaging and develop an e-commerce platform.

50 ADB. Bangladesh: Microenterprise Development Project.

CSOs are target groups and a direct link to hard-to-reach project beneficiaries at the community level. In Sri Lanka, with the Ministry of Finance as the implementing agency, the Small and Medium-Sized Enterprises Line of Credit Project provides financial assistance to small and medium-sized enterprises (SMEs) through 10 participating financial institutions.[51] The loan is provided exclusively to target underserved SMEs in productive sectors mainly for their capital investment to accelerate business growth. The targeted underserved SMEs are women-led, first-time borrowers, lacking in collateral, and based outside Colombo, the capital city. The project has an attached TA for (i) developing innovative financial schemes for SMEs and promoting export-oriented cluster development (funded by the JFPR), and (ii) developing an ecosystem for women entrepreneurship in Sri Lanka funded by the Women Entrepreneurs Finance Initiative. Civil society engagement takes place at two levels, with two chambers of commerce (the National Chamber of Commerce of Sri Lanka and the Federation of Chamber of Commerce of Sri Lanka) and tea societies as implementation partners. Gender-related capacity enhancement of the two chambers will improve the service delivery for target groups (the SMEs) and through tea societies by linking hard-to-reach, community-based tea smallholders as beneficiaries.

The project steering committee includes representatives from the chambers of commerce who directly contribute to project decision-making. They promote bank credit lines to their member companies and encourage their partners to borrow through advertisements, roadshows, and gatherings. The chambers also provided information about industries during the COVID-19 pandemic when many were in flux, and shared insights on other SMEs in the country. Since the project also supports the Government of Sri Lanka to promote women's entrepreneurship through the Women Entrepreneurs Finance Initiative, the women's groups in the chambers will provide a mentoring and networking facility through an online platform for women and training women entrepreneurs. As part of these interventions, ADB worked with women's chambers of commerce, the Institute of Certified Management Accountants of Sri Lanka, and other industrial associations to disseminate the project to potential women beneficiaries.

The project also introduced a new credit line for tea smallholders to support their capital investments, including replanting and new planting. To disseminate the project and promote financial literacy trainings, the tea societies are considered to play a role in providing a link to hard-to-reach smallholders in communities. The project consulted not only tea smallholders but also CSOs that promote environmentally and socially responsible tea products in designing the credit line and associated capacity development TA. The consultations increased the design team's understanding of their relationships and activities with line ministries. Discussions also covered how the government delivers public services to tea smallholders through an online platform and how to improve gender-sensitive and climate-resilient practices by tea small holders through the interventions related to the credit line and the TA.

---

[51]   ADB. Sri Lanka: Small and Medium-Sized Enterprises Line of Credit Project.

TAKEAWAYS

- CSOs may be target groups or beneficiaries (direct or indirect) in SARD loans and grants.

- CSOs can help ADB increase impact by increasing the project reach, accessing hard-to-reach groups, and enhancing sustainability.

- ADB projects can facilitate the formation or strengthening of CSOs as target groups.

- Working with local CSOs can provide added benefits to project implementation, such as a mechanism for the resolution of local issues.

- Involving CSOs as target groups or beneficiaries can increase the sustainability of a project and lead to better development outcomes.

- CSOs use participatory approaches, which by nature are inclusive, and strive to encompass different and intersecting groups.

- Engaging CSOs at the earliest stages of project design and maintaining that engagement throughout implementation and monitoring increases CSO ownership and results in sustainable outcomes.

Civil Society Organization Engagement in Technical Assistance

Technical assistance with CSO engagement is particularly appropriate for projects focusing on excluded and vulnerable communities. ADB administers TA to help DMCs plan and implement projects and improve knowledge and regional cooperation. The first case study in this section showcases how three CSOs are engaged by ADB to work on male engagement in gender equality and women's empowerment. The second is a demonstration project piloting the Graduation approach in Tamil Nadu in India and emphasizes how CSOs are suitable partners in exploratory and demonstration initiatives. The final case study focuses on the importance SARD placed on CSO engagement in developing a framework for GESI.

CSOs provide unique perspectives to help ADB focus on male engagement in gender equality and women's empowerment. Men and boys have a key role in achieving gender equality and women's empowerment and CSO expertise helps ADB understand the entry points for action by men and boys on gender equality in its portfolio in South Asia. Over 2021–2022, a consortium of three CSOs, the International Center for Research on Women,

MenEngage and Promundo, will do a stocktaking of initiatives for male engagement in gender equality in six countries in South Asia under an ADB-financed TA.[52] The ICRW–MenEngage–Promundo consortium supports strengthening the capacity of governments in Bangladesh, Bhutan, India, Maldives, Nepal, and Sri Lanka to pursue gender equality and women's empowerment through male engagement.

Concepts of masculinity, gender stereotypes, and traditional gender norms hamper men's ability to address gender barriers. Engaging boys and men in the process of achieving gender equality is a relatively underexplored but growing area of inquiry and has the potential to provide a much-needed step-change in accelerating progress in gender equality across South Asia. Considering their roles and privileges in perpetuating gender inequality, men need to be engaged in women's empowerment as accountable allies but also through the lens of co-beneficiaries, released from rigid gender norms and concepts of patriarchal masculinities and femininities.

Three CSOs will study male engagement across different levels: individual, family and household, community, institutional and organizational, and policy across several sectors (social, agriculture, infrastructure, and financial management). CSOs will consider the role of male engagement within the framework of multiple and intersecting inequalities (e.g., being elderly, from a marginalized caste, living in a remote area). They will take stock and prepare knowledge products on current initiatives by organizations, forums, and networks on male engagement in gender equality and women's empowerment in South Asia. They will also provide guidance and recommendations for entry points for ADB SARD and partner governments to promote male engagement in gender equality and women's empowerment and the transformation of masculinities within ADB's sector operations.[53]

Innovative CSO models can be tested at scale through pilot and demonstration activities. In 2021, ADB approved a $150 million loan to the Government of India to provide access to inclusive, resilient, and sustainable housing for the urban poor in Tamil Nadu. The loan comes with a $1.5 million TA project, which includes support to pilot the Graduation approach for vulnerable relocated communities. The Graduation approach is being adapted to the resettlement context in this project. Insights from its implementation may be used in other cities in India and the region.

ADB and the government designed the Inclusive, Resilient, and Sustainable Housing for Urban Poor Sector Project in Tamil Nadu while working with NGOs BRAC and World Vision India.[54] BRAC, the pioneer for the Graduation approach in Bangladesh, provided design support, presented the concept, and provided specialist expertise. ADB engaged World Vision India under the regional TA on Deepening Civil Society Engagement for Development Effectiveness Subproject 2 as Graduation experts to support the technical component on the project's preparation of two pilot subproject sites. World Vision India worked with the Tamil Nadu Urban Habitat Development Board on preparatory activities in the two pilot sites before relocation.

---

52 ADB. Regional: Supporting the Operational Priority 1 Agenda: Strengthening Poverty and Social Analysis.
53 Case study by H. D. Sudarshana A. Jayasundara, senior social development officer (gender), ADB Sri Lanka Resident Mission.
54 ADB. India: Inclusive, Resilient, and Sustainable Housing for Urban Poor Sector Project in Tamil Nadu.

The Graduation approach is a holistic, time-bound, sequenced set of interventions to help lift households out of poverty.[55] The sequencing of the interventions is important to strengthening individual capacities that will allow people to move beyond social assistance programs and build confidence in their ability to take control of their futures. What is innovative about the project is that it builds the institutional capacity of the Tamil Nadu Urban Habitat Development Board to implement a tailored Graduation program.

ADB recruited World Vision India competitively using the consultant qualification selection approach. Despite difficulties, including the spike in COVID-19 in India in the second quarter of 2021 and state elections from March to May 2021, the CSO started the assignment and selected households for the program, conducted orientation sessions on the Graduation program, and organized community communication meetings. The CSO has completed a market assessment, which identified a menu of feasible livelihood options for the relocated beneficiaries and a training plan. Outcomes from applying the Graduation approach in the two subproject pilots will likely inform the design of similar interventions for the project's seven other sites.

CSO perspectives help shape SARD's new approach to gender equality and social inclusion. The situation in the SARD member countries demands that GESI be pursued to ensure that intersecting inequalities experienced by women and excluded and vulnerable groups are reduced. Inequalities are most often based on gender, age, disability, social identities (e.g., caste, ethnicity), sexual and gender identities, geographic location, and income status. "Excluded" people experience systemic disadvantages while the "vulnerable" are those who experience situational disadvantage. Gender inequality is a core element of all forms of exclusion and vulnerability, with women of disadvantaged groups (e.g., women with disabilities, of caste or ethnic minority groups, older women) experiencing compounded barriers. The SARD GESI framework recognizes the multiple layers of disadvantage arising from intersectionality and intersecting identities. Hence, the rationale of the GESI framework are to understand and to identify who are the excluded and vulnerable, the causes, and existing responses; to empower for livelihood and voice empowerment; and to include, that is, to reduce discriminatory formal and informal policies and systems.

ADB's consultant organized virtual consultations with CSOs from January to July 2021 in the six SARD DMCs to gather inputs and insights for the SARD Framework on Gender Equality and Social Inclusion.[56] The civil society consultations aimed to share experiences of different categories of excluded and vulnerable groups. CSOs discussed barriers and capacities, good practices and lessons, and suggestions for SARD's GESI framework and GESI mainstreaming in future projects.

ADB's consultant engaged 65 CSOs, 47 NGOs (at least 1 advocacy and identity-based NGO per excluded and vulnerable category), 11 external development partners, and 7 key

55   ADB. 2021. Technical Assistance to India for Supporting Capacity for Affordable Housing Delivery. See also: P. Rawal. 2019. *What is the Graduation Approach?* Asian Development Blog.
56   This was part of PricewaterhouseCoopers Pvt. Ltd. (PwC India)'s assignment under TA 9896 REG: Supporting the Operational Priority 1 Agenda: Strengthening Poverty and Social Analysis-Strengthening Social Inclusion Impacts of SARD Operations (53102-001).

resource persons from academia or leaders in their field in the DMCs. Selecting NGOs, donor agencies, and resource persons involved first reviewing their websites and assessing their experience, links with government, and willingness to participate.[57] The consultant also asked specific interest-group NGOs to include community participants in the consultations to capture their real-life experiences. Sharing initiatives that addressed barriers and lessons from unsuccessful interventions enriched the discussions.

During these consultations, the participants validated the three domains of change or pillars of the Leave-No-One-Behind framework of the Department for International Development of the United Kingdom guide as a useful structure for analyzing barriers to and opportunities for GESI and designing responsive actions. These elements are (i) understand for action, (ii) empower for change, (iii) include for opportunity. The experiences shared by the groups regarding the issues and agency of women, older persons, persons with disabilities, LGBTI+ community, people in remote and difficult to reach areas, and people with poor income status reinforced the understanding that for GESI to be achieved, SARD must understand these three domains of change.[58]

TAKEAWAYS

- TA provides ADB with opportunities to pilot initiatives or demonstration activities with CSOs which, if successful, can be incorporated into the loan or grant.
- A TA with CSO engagement is appropriate for projects focusing on engagement with excluded and vulnerable communities.
- CSOs can bring new approaches and perspectives, which can be piloted in the TA.
- Selecting CSOs with experience in working with excluded and vulnerable groups will help build trust with local communities and key stakeholders.
- CSOs can provide services as consultants on a TA or be the beneficiaries of these approaches.
- Orienting CSOs to ADB and government processes at the point of procurement allows for smoother engagement during project implementation (e.g., how CSOs should engage with the community during elections).

---

[57] In India, the consultant reviewed each shortlisted organization for their work with the Government of India to ensure that they had the experience working with the government and were not blacklisted.
[58] By Francesco Tornieri, principal social development specialist (gender and development), South Asia Department.

●●●●

Monitoring and Evaluation

SARD has an opportunity to increase CSO engagement in monitoring and evaluation. ADB's long-term corporate strategy specifically commits ADB to strengthen engagement with CSOs in monitoring projects.[59] There are few examples of CSOs involved in monitoring and evaluation of ADB operations in South Asia. However, CSOs are particularly well-placed to monitor ADB projects as they are independent of ADB and the government. Strategy 2030's Operational Priority 6 outlines the value that CSO engagement brings, particularly in terms of strengthening social accountability, improving service delivery, and enhancing transparency. CSOs are one conduit for citizen engagement, and experience shows that CSO engagement increases inclusiveness by placing citizens, particularly the excluded and vulnerable, at the center of the development process.[60]

CSO engagement in monitoring ADB-financed operations in South Asia is an opportunity for SARD and ADB to strengthen CSO engagement. Several project planning documents indicate some contracting of CSOs to undertake project monitoring as part of their other tasks. Some projects showcased in this report included monitoring activities for CSOs, particularly the additional financing for the Bangladesh Southwest Area Integrated Water Resources Planning and Management Project, where water management groups monitor project interventions. Other projects included planned CSO engagement for monitoring projects, particularly around safeguards and monitoring resettlement plans.

Under the Secondary Towns Urban Development Project in Bhutan (approved in June 2018), the project team engaged an NGO in May 2021, 3 years after approval, to monitor the GAP implementation.[61] The NGO's role is to conduct the baseline survey and end-of-project impact survey to assess the outcomes and impacts of the GAP, to ensure that all GAP activities are implemented, to mobilize stakeholder participation in GAP implementation, and report progress and results.

Beyond engagement as a consultant or service provider, there are few examples of CSOs monitoring or evaluating projects voluntarily as independent entities. The team identified only one project, the Sri Lanka Wind Power Generation Project, where the NGO Forum on ADB monitors this project. Voluntary monitoring and evaluation by CSOs is another area where CSO engagement could be strengthened. Taking the Sri Lanka Wind Power Generation Project case study as an example, CSO monitoring can add value to ADB-financed operations. Project monitoring strengthens accountability, improves transparency, and increases citizen engagement.

---

[59]   ADB. 2018. *Strategy 2030: Achieving a Prosperous, Inclusive, Resilient, and Sustainable Asia and the Pacific*. Manila. page vii.

[60]   ADB. 2019. *Strategy 2030 Operational Plan for Priority 6: Strengthening Governance and Institutional Capacity, 2019–2024*. Manila.

[61]   ADB. Bhutan: Secondary Towns Urban Development Project.

TAKEAWAYS

- There are relatively few examples of CSOs involved in monitoring and evaluation in ADB operations in South Asia and this is an opportunity for SARD to strengthen its engagement with CSOs, and through CSOs, citizens.

- CSO engagement in project monitoring can improve transparency and accountability.

- ADB can engage CSOs for project monitoring or CSOs can monitor voluntarily.

- Developing CSO capacity for monitoring ADB-financed projects and other government initiatives could help boost CSO and citizen engagement.

5

Policy Level

ADB has committed to engaging with CSOs on major policy design and reviews.

SARD can increase CSO engagement in upstream policy dialogue. ADB has committed to engaging with CSOs on major policy design and reviews. This section examines recent major policies through the lens of engagement with CSOs in South Asia, particularly the development of Strategy 2030 and other recent ADB flagship policies. There is an opportunity for ADB to build on its extensive engagement with CSOs in developing Strategy 2030 and translating this experience of participation to other major policy development and review programs. ADB's CSO sourcebook provides tips and guidelines for engaging CSOs in policy formulation and review and CSO engagement in CPS formulation.[62]

South Asian CSOs engage in the road to Strategy 2030. In July 2018, ADB's Board of Directors approved a new long-term corporate strategy—Strategy 2030: Achieving a Prosperous, Inclusive, Resilient, and Sustainable Asia and the Pacific.[63] ADB developed Strategy 2030 in consultation with member governments, policy makers, academics, CSOs, and the ADB Board and staff. ADB produced a consultation plan and associated website, the Road to 2030. ADB then held consultations throughout the Asia and Pacific region and beyond involving 73 activities in different parts of the world. ADB consulted with 1,150 individual stakeholders.[64]

---

62 ADB. 2021. *A Sourcebook for Engaging with Civil Society Organizations in Asian Development Bank Operations*. Manila.

63 ADB. 2018. *Strategy 2030: Achieving a Prosperous, Inclusive, Resilient, and Sustainable Asia and the Pacific*. Manila.

64 ADB. Strategy 2030 preparation process.

In South Asia, ADB held consultations in Colombo, Sri Lanka from 29 February to 1 March 2016, and 11–12 August 2016 in Delhi, India. In the Colombo consultations, ADB consulted representatives from CARE International, the Center for Women's Research, the Consortium for Humanitarian Agencies, Sarvodaya, Women in Logistics and Transport, World University Service of Canada, and others. In the Delhi consultations, participants included ActionAid India, Aga Khan Foundation, Center for Social Research, India Development Foundation, Transparency International India, and others.

In these two consultations, CSOs provided inputs to the Road to 2030 report and raised issues about CSO engagement with ADB and member governments. A report from the India consultations noted that "ADB's modalities for engaging with civil society institutions need more clarity. More direct interaction between ADB and civil society is needed to clarify partnership modalities and priorities. ADB should provide grant-based and soft loan assistance to civil society institutions. Partnerships with youth are critical for their intellectual and professional development. Even where jobs are available, the employability potential of the youth is weak due to lack of skills and inadequate preparedness to enter the job market."[65]

ADB held an additional consultation for Strategy 2030 with CSOs at ADB's headquarters in Manila in November 2016. Representatives from several CSOs from South Asia attended, including the Bangladesh Women's Chamber of Commerce and Industry, Hand in Hand (India), Nari Maitree (Bangladesh), Rural Education and Development (Bhutan), Tarayana Foundation (Bhutan), and others. At this consultation, participants broke into groups to consider issues related to ADB's mission, strategic priorities, business areas and the overall ADB value proposition. CSO participants raised several issues, such as the following:

- CSOs ought to be involved much earlier at the CPS formulation and at the project planning stages to enable checks and balances at the programming, project planning, and design phases. Evaluation upon project completion will then benefit from qualitative and quantitative measures as CSOs monitor the intended outputs.
- There was a limited level of engagement with CSOs in Strategy 2030 because ADB did not circulate a formal document in advance of the consultations and requested that the draft Strategy 2030 document be shared with clear deadlines for comments and that the matrix of comments (particularly those involved in policy review and monitoring) also be shared.[66]

CSO engagement during the Energy Policy Review. During ADB's Energy Policy Review, ADB sought inputs from CSOs across the Asia and Pacific region. An advocacy CSO raised concerns about the consultative approach used for the review.[67] Notwithstanding, at ADB's virtual 54th Annual Meeting in May 2021, the NGO Forum on ADB hosted an online, Asia

---

65 ADB. 2016. *Consultations with Stakeholders from India on "Road to 2030": ADB's New Strategy Note-to-File*.
66 ADB. 2016. *Consultations with Civil Society Organizations on "Road to 2030": ADB's New Strategy 21 November 2016, Auditorium B, ADB Headquarters - Note-to-File*.
67 Concerns raised by the NGO Forum on ADB included the 2-week window for consultation on the 2021 Energy Policy Working Paper, the lack of translation into major regional languages, including Hindi, and the lack of availability of the working paper for the vision-impaired. NGO Forum on ADB. NGO Forum on ADB's Critique of the ADB's 2021 Energy Policy Working Paper.

and the Pacific regional forum on Reviewing ADB's Energy Policy to Meet the Paris Goal of 1.5 Degrees Celsius, indicating ADB's openness to engaging with CSOs on this issue.[68]

TAKEAWAYS

- An opportunity for strengthening ADB engagement with CSOs in South Asia is in upstream planning, particularly policy dialogue.

- A clear stakeholder engagement and consultation plan, informed by stakeholder mapping which includes CSOs, guides engagement on policy review. This consultation plan should be shared with stakeholders so the process is transparent.

- Providing CSOs with appropriate timeframes and translating major draft policy papers into national languages will enhance CSO engagement in policy design and review.

---

[68] ADB. 54th Annual Meeting of the Board of Governors Virtual 3–5 May 2021. Reviewing ADB's Energy Policy to Meet the Paris Goal of 1.5 Degrees Celsius.

6

Lessons and Recommendations

More meaningful engagement of CSOs at the project design stage is needed, and will lead to improved levels of CSO participation during project implementation.

Where is SARD engaging with CSOs? The analysis of the SARD portfolio demonstrates that SARD is working with CSOs across a range of sectors including agriculture and natural resources, environmental and social safeguards, water supply and sanitation, gender equality, education and skills development, transport, urban development, social inclusion, and climate change and disaster risk management.

Where is SARD performing well in CSO engagement? SARD is performing well in engaging CSOs in project implementation, most notably as consultants, contractors, and service providers, but also as target groups and beneficiaries. SARD is adopting some innovative and novel approaches (e.g., using the Graduation approach to enhance resettlement plans, working with CSOs on men's engagement in women's empowerment, CSOs delivering microloans as a form of emergency assistance, developing a new and transformative GESI framework, and working with local networks of CSOs to enhance community coordination in urban development and water and sanitation).

SARD is using conventional approaches to great effect. Examples include the use of local CSOs for assistance in safeguards delivery, GAP or GESI action plan implementation, and the continued engagement with private sector representative CSOs such as chambers of commerce or industry associations.

This report showcases good practices and approaches that are boosting the results of the department, leading to high levels of CSO engagement over 2015–2021. The learning showcased in this report is relevant to other ADB operations departments and provides a template for engagement that can be applied to further strengthening ADB's work with CSOs.

Lessons: Where could SARD improve on CSO engagement? SARD could improve by engaging with CSOs earlier in the project cycle and involving them more in monitoring and evaluating ADB-financed operations. Partly in recognition of the globally shrinking civil society space over the past 10 years (footnote 5), more opportunities are needed for advocacy and identity-based CSOs to engage with ADB-financed operations in South Asia. This support is needed across the region. A summary of lessons from ADB staff, CSOs, and project documents follows.

Early CSO engagement leads to meaningful engagement and other benefits. One of the strongest themes to come out of this report is the need to engage CSOs early in project preparation. Survey respondents and interviewees both commented on the benefits of early CSO engagement, such as (i) engaging with CSOs as potential beneficiaries to improve project design, (ii) improved engagement with communities on project design, (iii) helping project teams validate issues and collect baseline data, (iv) gaining community support for project objectives, and (v) creating trusted relationships between CSOs and project teams to improve implementation. Improved development outcomes and positive design changes can arise from CSO engagement, as illustrated in the Sri Lanka Wind Power Generation Project case study where ADB engaged with CSOs as advocacy organizations.

CSO engagement in monitoring and evaluation and upstream policy dialogue is a missed opportunity. ADB's Strategy 2030 states ADB "will strengthen collaboration with civil society organizations in designing, implementing, and monitoring projects" (footnote 59). ADB's Operational Plan for Priority 6 states: "ADB will work in partnership with a broad range of CSOs to strengthen social accountability and contribute to responsive service delivery in DMCs" (footnote 60). Despite this clear mandate, the team did not find significant evidence of CSO engagement in monitoring and evaluation in SARD and notes an opportunity for increased regional engagement on policy dialogue. The nature of CSOs, particularly how these organizations use culturally sensitive approaches to improve citizens' lives, places them in a unique position to ensure that a diverse array of citizen voices are heard.

Building ADB and government skills in CSO identification and due diligence will benefit projects. The report finds that ADB SARD and government staff need help identifying appropriate CSOs and conducting due diligence and financial assessments of CSOs for potential engagement. Project teams also need additional support to enhance meaningful CSO engagement.

" **CSOs should be given capacity-building opportunities to become part of development.**

— *Respondent from survey on ADB's CSO engagement in South Asia*

Developing CSO capacity selectively is required for more effective engagement with ADB. Respondents indicated that CSOs need to be able to engage more effectively with ADB and government teams. CSO understanding of ADB's business model, procurement methods, and project cycle may be limited. However, capacity development can mean different things to different stakeholders and any capacity support initiative must be tailored to the context. For example, in Bhutan, advocacy and identity-based CSOs have specific needs for capacity development. Under one ADB-financed project, only one CSO bid for a role in the project even though ADB expected many CSO bids. In another program in Bhutan, the DPOB helps the government but voluntarily. Other development partners recognize the capacity gap in Bhutan.[69] Selective CSO capacity development is needed to increase the effectiveness of ADB and CSO engagement.

Raising awareness about existing flexible options for CSO procurement will improve procurement outcomes. Several ADB staff noted the lack of specialized recruitment and contracting processes for CSO engagement. The time needed to recruit CSOs is also an issue of concern. This has been raised in earlier reports, including the 2015 study. ADB's Procurement Policy 2017 allows much greater flexibility for CSO procurement but many ADB staff and project teams continue using approaches they are familiar with. The revised CSO sourcebook released in December 2021 provides useful advice and guidance on innovative approaches to procurement, particularly for recruiting small CSOs. ADB needs to consider raising awareness among ADB staff and DMC officials about the flexible options for CSO procurement that already exist and encourage staff and project teams to use the most suitable method for their project's requirements.

Budgets for CSO activities and engagement can be inadequate and affect results. Participants mentioned the inadequate budgets sometimes allocated for CSO activities, which has led to quality concerns about CSO deliverables. Several project teams made this point. Budgets for CSO activities must be sufficient to cover the activities they are expected to perform.

Gaps remain between engineering and community engagement activities. According to some participants, the focus of government agencies during project design is often on infrastructure or the "hardware" in project loans. Sometimes this extends to project implementation and a gap emerges between the project engineers and the CSOs engaged to perform community relations and other "soft skill" activities. In some projects, there appears to be a gap in understanding between project engineers and PMU staff in the

---

[69] European Union. 2019. Action Document for Promoting Good Governance – support to Civil Society and Bhutanese Parliament engagement with civil society organizations (CSOs); UNDP. 2020. *UNDP Bhutan Governance Multi-Year Framework 2020–2023*.

executing agency or the contractor and the CSOs performing community engagement activities. Often, participants said this gap narrows once the CSO starts work and the PMU staff see the value the CSO brings, particularly in resolving local conflicts and complaints.

Clear documentation of CSO roles in project documents results in better outcomes. ADB must ensure CSO roles are well-documented and expectations clearly detailed, particularly in terms of reference and in consultation and participation plans. ADB and government agencies can reduce misunderstandings on all sides by involving CSOs earlier in the project design and documenting roles well. Pre-bid meetings can also be used to provide clarity to CSOs. Several projects reviewed for this report had extremely detailed terms of reference for CSOs, which provided the clarity they needed to perform their roles successfully.

CSOs need support to learn ADB and government processes. Some ADB staff reported challenges related to CSOs' lack of understanding of ADB or government policies and processes. This extended from procurement through to project implementation. Several interviewees reported CSOs asking for changes to contractual terms based on a misunderstanding about time-based contracts and a lack of effective advance financing. This led to some issues in implementing projects. CSOs generally prefer output-based contracts because of the reduced administrative burden, need advance financing because of their limited cash resources, and struggle to prepare and submit claims with proper documentation for time-based contracts. This issue requires specialist training and attention toward sensitizing CSOs to these policies and processes at the point of procurement.

> **"**
> **ADB should hold regular high-level NGO forums and meetings at the national level with government officials [to help raise awareness on the benefits of working with NGOs and CSOs].**
>
> — *Respondent from survey on ADB's CSO engagement in South Asia*

Government–CSO project collaboration results in stronger relations and mutual understanding. ADB staff and CSO representatives raised a concern that in some, but not all cases, there is hesitation among government staff to engage CSOs on projects. These concerns are compounded in different countries by historical relations with CSOs, the politicization of CSOs, and relations with advocacy CSOs. In some situations after recruitment, the CSOs and ADB staff felt the CSOs had to prove themselves to be capable, even after winning an assignment in a competitive selection. Participants reported some of these issues subsided once the project got underway and the CSO demonstrated its capability and worth to the project. This highlights how CSO engagement early in the project would be useful and the need to encourage regular interaction between ADB, CSOs, and the government.

Engaging CSOs early in project design can help bring about significant change and get all stakeholders on board with the social aspects of the project. See for example where ADB and the government designed the Inclusive, Resilient, and Sustainable Housing for Urban Poor Sector Project in Tamil Nadu working with NGOs BRAC and World Vision.

Recommendations. Based on the 10 lessons emerging from this review, the team recommends five main actions for SARD and notes that other departments may also benefit from the learning in the SARD portfolio and implementing these recommendations.

RECOMMENDATION 1

Invest in early CSO engagement.

The findings indicate that more meaningful engagement of CSOs at the project design stage is needed and will lead to improved levels of CSO participation during project implementation. Evidence shows that CSO engagement early in project design can introduce innovations and strengthen the social dimensions of the project. ADB needs to invest more in early CSO engagement. A TA facility may be an ideal vehicle to ensure effective, productive, and sustainable partnerships among government, ADB, and CSOs. A TA facility would allow for scoping CSOs as consultants, service providers, and partners at the design stage, and assist governments with capacity development actions to sustainably engage with CSOs.[70] This report recommends that SARD identify two or three pipeline projects in each DMC where CSO engagement could be strengthened. Comprehensive stakeholder mapping should be used to identify CSOs with expertise relevant to these projects and any capacity development needs of CSOs and government should be identified. Specific capacity development for CSOs and government to enhance CSO engagement for each project could be supported. Engaging advocacy and identity-based CSOs in South Asia is a particular area where ADB could increase its investment in early engagement with CSOs. Appendix 4 outlines how this could be achieved through a regional TA facility.

RECOMMENDATION 2

Enhance CSO knowledge on ADB and government procurement and contracting processes.

Train CSOs to use the CMS. ADB's CMS is challenging for CSOs to navigate and they need support. ADB should provide CSOs with training in multiple formats in multiple languages and via multiple channels (e.g., short, self-paced e-learning modules that can be taken via smartphone or tablet; YouTube videos that walk CSOs through establishing an account and expressing interest; hard copy pamphlets or guides for CSOs that explain step-by-step how to register and bid). This will also help the private sector in accessing and using the CMS. A CSO could be engaged to ensure these materials answer common questions and are easy to understand.

---

70 ADB. 2022. *Staff Instruction on Business Processes for Transaction Technical Assistance (Sovereign)*. Manila.

Familiarize CSOs with procurement and contracting processes. ADB should provide tailored training and guidance in local languages on ADB and government processes at the point of procurement for CSOs. This training should be tailored to CSOs and the project, and cover issues such as contract management, reporting requirements (including the provision of reporting templates), making claims and documentation, advance financing, subcontracting, milestone submission and payments, engaging with the government on permissions to enter certain areas or consulting with certain groups at particular times (i.e., during elections). These costs should be built into the project budget or incorporated into the regional TA facility proposed under Recommendation 1.

Use innovative procurement methods for CSOs. This report does not recommend changes to ADB's procurement processes to accommodate CSOs. ADB's procurement processes are based on sound principles of good governance designed to promote accountability and transparency and prevent fraud and corruption. ADB's CSO sourcebook describes how CSOs can be engaged in many innovative ways within the established ADB procurement processes. This report has not covered these innovative procurement approaches as these are addressed in the CSO sourcebook (e.g., community participation in procurement, engaging a large CSO to subcontract smaller community-based CSOs or people's organizations).

Avoid the least-cost selection method for procurement of CSOs unless the assignment is genuinely standard, small, and routine. Participants reported that some governments in South Asia prefer using the least-cost selection method for safeguards implementation assignments. The method should be used only for small assignments of a standard or routine nature (audits, engineering design and supervision of simple projects, and simple surveys) where there are well-established practices and standards.[71] The complex area of safeguards plan implementation, with its variety, human element, and significant potential to delay project implementation, does not fit this category. Avoid using least-cost selection for safeguards.

Use output-based contracts for CSOs and ensure that adequate funds are advanced for CSOs to conduct project activities. CSOs prefer output-based contracts rather than time-based contracts. CSO accounting systems are more suited to output-based contracts and they are easier to administer. CSOs, unlike commercial consulting firms, will not likely have reserve funds to fund activities for retroactive payment and will need a positive cash flow. Ensure there are regular milestones for the CSO activities and that the first tranche of funds is advanced on signing the contract. On the achievement of one milestone, advance funds promptly for the next.

Ensure clear documentation of CSO roles in project planning documents. Ensure that CSOs understand what they are agreeing to and that the project team crafts terms of reference with appropriate deliverables, milestone dates, and inputs suitable to the CSO tasks. Prepare consultation and participation plans with comprehensive stakeholder mapping and analysis that clearly outline the roles for CSOs and the costs associated with their participation.

---

71 ADB. 2017. *Procurement Regulations for ADB Borrowers: Good, Works, Nonconsulting, and Consulting Services.* Manila.

Participation plans are required if the summary poverty reduction and social strategy (a mandatory annex to the report and recommendation of the President) indicates that the project has planned meaningful CSO engagement.[72] A participation plan is mandatory where there is meaningful CSO engagement planned and should be linked to relevant project documents and resources to help ensure the planned participation of CSOs and the poor and vulnerable in project implementation is delivered. A CSO participation plan may be embedded within the GAP, GESI action plans, or safeguards documents only if all planned CSO engagement is already documented there. SARD should observe this requirement. ADB should consider including consultation and participation plan adherence as a loan or grant covenant, under Schedule 4 (Execution of Project; Environmental, Social, Financial and Other Matters) of loan and/or grant agreements.

RECOMMENDATION 3

Increase CSO roles in monitoring and evaluation.

Few CSOs engage with ADB in monitoring ADB-financed operations in South Asia. Beyond CSOs monitoring minor activities under safeguards, GAP, or GESI action plan implementation, and the work of advocacy groups such as the NGO Forum on ADB, this report found few exemplars of South Asian CSOs monitoring ADB-financed operations in South Asia either independently or in a contracted capacity. There may be more examples but the researchers did not find any.

CSOs could be engaged to monitor aspects of ADB-financed projects, such as GAP or GESI action plan implementation or for results-based lending, e.g., verification of disbursement-linked indicators. CSOs often use participatory approaches and simple tools to monitor service delivery including social audits, citizen report cards, digital storytelling, and citizen dashboards. ADB should provide support to CSOs to fulfill these roles of providing third-party monitoring of ADB-financed loans, grants, and TA. These approaches have the added benefit of increasing citizen engagement in monitoring government service delivery. ADB could incorporate this capacity development for monitoring as a specific activity under the regional TA facility (proposed above) or as stand-alone support, including specific capacity development for the use of technology-based monitoring and data collection and analysis tools. ADB could support CSOs to monitor ADB-financed operations as paid consultants or service providers or to conduct monitoring activities voluntarily. ADB and governments should encourage CSOs to perform these roles either during implementation (for monitoring) or immediately after implementation (without significant delay), to effectively capture good practice and lessons.

At the project design stage, ADB project teams should assess CSOs' monitoring capacity and budget for their capacity development and involvement in these roles.

---

[72]   Refer to Appendix 1 for the definition of "planned meaningful CSO engagement."

Encourage regular interaction among CSOs, ADB, and the government at country level, outside the project cycle.

One issue that appears to hinder engagement between government, ADB, and CSO stakeholders is "unfamiliarity." There is a need to enhance relationships among ADB, CSOs, and government and more effectively bringing CSO specialist knowledge into ADB. Forming country-level ADB–government–CSO tripartite sector groups, if nonexistent, or a CSO country advisory group for the ADB resident mission, will go a long way to CSOs getting to know ADB and the government, and vice versa. In addition, invite CSOs to present their experiences at ADB and government planning events to allow government officials and ADB staff to identify which CSOs have the capacities they need and could add value to ADB-financed projects. CSOs want to showcase their expertise, yet CSOs report they sometimes feel that their engagement with government and ADB is a "one-way street" (i.e., ADB and government to CSO). Good practice and knowledge sharing are benefits of encouraging this tripartite interaction. ADB can play a strategic role in encouraging this engagement among ADB, government, and CSOs.

Increase the engagement of CSOs in upstream policy dialogue.

ADB should conduct comprehensive stakeholder mapping in the early stages of policy formulation or review, prepare clear consultation plans with stakeholders, and share these in advance. ADB should share draft policies or draft CPSs before consultations, translated into appropriate national languages, with ample time for sharing comments so stakeholders can make meaningful and specific comments on proposals. During online consultations, CSOs from specific regions are often not convened together, as consultations focus on topics, not geographic proximity; however, ADB should consider how CSOs may contribute to the policy dialogue process beyond seeking their inputs as key stakeholders. For example, can CSOs facilitate in-country discussions or assist in preparing consultation plans or stakeholder mapping? COVID-19 requires special approaches to CSO engagement in policy dialogue since face-to-face consultations may not always be possible. It is important to think about who may be excluded if consultations are only online.

These recommendations build on the work that ADB is undertaking to enhance engagement with CSOs across South Asia and the broader Asia and Pacific region. By working with CSOs in ways they can appreciate and adapt to, ADB can facilitate CSOs' meaningful contributions to ADB's vision for a prosperous, inclusive, resilient, and sustainable Asia and the Pacific.

APPENDIX 1

ADB's Revised Civil Society Organization Engagement Indicator

Starting in 2020, Asian Development Bank (ADB) changed the way it measures and reports on civil society organization (CSO) engagement in ADB operations. ADB previously measured the proportion of all approved projects that *planned* to include CSO engagement in a year. Under a new CSO engagement indicator approved in 2020, ADB now reports the percentage of *completed* projects that delivered meaningful CSO engagement as a proportion of the total number of completed projects which had planned to do so. ADB defines "meaningful CSO engagement" as significant information sharing or consultation activities or any type of collaboration or partnership with CSOs.[1]

As part of the project preparation process, ADB staff and member governments complete a poverty and social analysis. This is summarized in a project document called the Summary Poverty Reduction and Social Strategy, a mandatory appendix to the report and recommendation of the President. Part II of the strategy is focused on Participation and Empowering the Poor. In this section, project teams are asked to indicate the level of CSO engagement planned in the project. In recent versions of the strategy template, teams are asked to rate civil society engagement across four approaches to participation: information generation and sharing, consultation, collaboration, and partnership. Each of these is rated *low, medium, high* or *not applicable*. A high rating for information generation and sharing and/or a high rating for consultation and/or any rating (low, medium, or high) for collaboration or partnership classifies the project as having planned meaningful civil society engagement.

In practice, this means engagement with CSOs is robust, purposeful, and potentially transformative. For example, meaningful consultation could encompass focus group discussions or participatory workshops with CSOs and the feedback integrated into the project design or implementation. Collaboration may mean a CSO has a direct role in a project and has some control over decision-making. Distributing flyers to CSOs, preparing a project website, and hosting occasional information meetings with CSOs does not constitute meaningful CSO engagement.

---

1   ADB. 2021. *Highlights of Cooperation with Civil Society Organizations*. Manila.

APPENDIX 2

ADB Projects in South Asia Featured in This Report

Project Number	Country	Project Name	Project Cost ($M)	ADB Financing ($M)	Date of Approval	Status as of Sep 2022
42466-016	BAN	Skills for Employment Investment Program - Tranche 2	128.50	100.00	24 Nov 2016	Active
34418-023	BAN	Southwest Area Integrated Water Resources Planning and Management Project – Additional Financing	63.70	45.00	30 Sep 2015	Active
51269-001	BAN	Microenterprise Development Project	125.00	100.00	26 Nov 2018	Active
50296-002	BHU	Skills Training and Education Pathways Upgradation Project	18.00	15.00	30 Aug 2018	Active
42229-016	BHU	Secondary Towns Urban Development Project	12.00	10.00	18 Jun 2018	Active
49107-006	IND	West Bengal Drinking Water Sector Improvement Project	349.00	240.00	29 Aug 2018	Active
38412-033	IND	Assam Integrated Flood and Riverbank Erosion Risk Management Investment Program Project 2	82.34	60.16	7 Dec 2018	Closed
44429-013	IND	Climate Adaptation in Vennar Subbasin in Cauvery Delta Project	144.00	100.00	7 Jun 2016	Closed
43574-025	IND	Uttar Pradesh Major District Roads Improvement Project	428.00	300.00	14 Apr 2016	Closed
53067-004 Supported by 50364-003 - TA 9592	IND	Inclusive, Resilient, and Sustainable Housing for Urban Poor Sector Project in Tamil Nadu REG - Deepening Civil Society Engagement for Development Effectiveness - Deepening ADB-Civil Society Engagement in Selected Countries in Southeast and South Asia (Subproject 2)	215.00 0.50	150.00 0.50	3 Sep 2021 19 Sep 2018	Active Closed
54373-001	MLD	Strengthening Gender Inclusive Initiatives Project	6.75	6.75		Proposed
51077-002	MLD	Greater Malé Environmental Improvement and Waste Management Project	40.00	33.07	28 Jun 2018	Active
43448-014	NEP	Bagmati River Basin Improvement Project - Additional Financing	78.80	63.00	20 Sep 2019	Active
49202	NEP	Disaster Risk Reduction and Livelihood Restoration for Earthquake-Affected Communities	17.80	15.00	7 Oct 2015	Closed
51190-001	NEP	Disaster Resilience of Schools Project	198.86	158.86	10 Sep 2018	Active
53102-001 TA 9896-REG	REG	Supporting the Operational Priority 1 Agenda: Strengthening Poverty and Social Analysis Supporting: Male Engagement in Promoting Gender Equality and Women's Empowerment	2.25	1.75	9 Dec 2019	Active
49345-002	SRI	Wind Power Generation Project	256.70	200.00	24 Oct 2017	Active
45148-008	SRI	Greater Colombo Water and Wastewater Management Improvement Investment Program (Tranche 3)	178.02	128.00	8 Dec 2015	Active
42251-019	SRI	Skills Sector Enhancement Program - Additional Financing	575.50	100.00	28 Mar 2018	Active
49273-001	SRI	Small and Medium-Sized Enterprises Line of Credit Project	374.44	340.00	15 Feb 2016	Active

ADB = Asian Development Bank, BAN = Bangladesh, BHU = Bhutan, IND = India, MLD = Maldives, NEP = Nepal, REG = regional, SRI = Sri Lanka.
Source: Asian Development Bank.

APPENDIX 3

ADB and CSO Staff Interviewed for This Report

Asian Development Bank Staff and Consultants

- Mohammad Rashed Al Hasan, senior project officer (Financial Sector), Bangladesh Resident Mission (BRM), South Asia Department (SARD)
- Gobinda Bar, senior external relations officer, BRM, SARD
- Ricardo Carlos Barba, principal safeguards specialist, SARD
- Saswati G. Belliappa, senior safeguards specialist, SARD
- Kamal Dahanayake, senior project officer, Urban and Water Supply Sanitation, Sri Lanka Resident Mission (SRLM), SARD
- Luca Di Mario, urban development specialist, SARD
- Vikas Goyal, senior project officer (water resources) India Resident Mission (INRM), SARD
- Smita Gyawali, senior project officer (education), Nepal Resident Mission (NRM), SARD
- Prathaj Haputhanthri, associate project officer (energy), SLRM, SARD
- Ryotaro Hayashi, social sector economist, SARD
- Takuya Hoshino, finance sector specialist, SARD
- Suraia Jabin, consultant, SARD
- H.D. Sudarshana A. Jayasundara, senior social development officer (gender), SLRM, SARD
- Binita Shah Khadka, senior external relations officer, NRM, SARD
- Jaimes Kolatharaj, senior energy specialist, SARD
- Jagir Kumar, senior project officer (transport), INRM, SARD
- Nilesh Kumar, associate environment officer, INRM, SARD
- Maria Laureen E. Laurito, social development specialist, SARD
- Zhigang Li, senior social sector specialist, SARD
- Sourav Majumder, senior project officer (urban), INRM, SARD
- Suzanne K. Marsh, water resources specialist, SARD
- Suhail Mircha, safeguards officer, INRM, SARD
- Pravash Kumar Mishra, senior safeguards officer, INRM, SARD
- Raghavendra Naduvinamani, project analyst, INRM, SARD
- Tshewang Norbu, portfolio management specialist, Bhutan Resident Mission (BHRM), SARD
- Mayumi Ozaki, senior financial sector specialist, SARD
- S.E. Ebadur Rahman, senior social sector officer (education and health), BRM, SARD
- Arun Shumshere Rana, senior project officer, NRM, SARD
- Sumeet Rathore, associate safeguards officer, INRM, SARD
- Nirojan Donald Sinclair, project officer infrastructure, SRLM, SARD
- Mukund Kumar Sinha, transport specialist, SARD
- Pushkar Srivastava, project management specialist, BRM, SARD
- Rajesh Yadav, senior project officer, Natural Resources and Agriculture, INRM SARD

Civil Society Organization Staff and Consultants

- Zameela Ahmed, country manager, Live and Learn Environmental Education, Maldives
- Hasanthi Jayasinghe, entrepreneurship expert, Oxfam Sri Lanka
- Navindra Liyanaarachchi, private sector expert, Oxfam Sri Lanka
- Prabha Pokhrel, team leader, Integrated Development Society Nepal
- Uttam Pudasaini, president, Bagmati Beautification Concern Platform, Nepal
- Rukmani Rathnayake, team leader, Oxfam, Sri Lanka
- Fathimath Thasneem, Live and Learn Environmental Education, Maldives

APPENDIX 4

Sample Terms of Reference for Regional Technical Assistance Facility

A Technical Assistance Special Fund Facility for Civil Society Engagement in the South Asia Department (SARD) of the Asian Development Bank (ADB) is established to support civil society organizations (CSOs) in implementing projects, grants, and technical assistance. The focus of the facility is to strengthen the capacity of CSO participation and engagements on the following priority sectors: agriculture and natural resources, gender equality and social inclusion, transport, and urban and water projects, that are matched with the demands of developing member countries (DMCs).

Outcomes from the technical assistance facility contributes to the Strategy 2030 commitment to strengthening CSO engagement and achieved through three outputs: (i) improved DMC systems and processes for CSO engagement at the project design stage, (ii) enhanced articulation of planned CSO engagement in project design documentation, and (iii) strengthened capacities of DMC officials and CSOs in engaging CSOs in ADB-financed operations.

Managed by a CSO, or a network for CSOs, with broad reach and links among different CSOs across ADB's DMCs, the roles of the facility manager are as follows:
- Create pathways for CSO engagement in project structures of DMC counterparts such as in project steering committees of executing and implementing agencies.
- Identify roles of CSOs in pipeline projects where they will add value, map, and scope potential CSOs that can perform those roles.
- Conduct market scans and identify suitable CSOs to perform those roles.
- Conduct preliminary fiduciary and/or financial assessments of identified CSOs.[1]
- Conduct capacity assessments and training needs analyses of CSOs and DMC staff to foster improved CSO engagement in ADB-financed operations.
- Develop the capacity of specific CSOs and DMC executing and implementing agency staff to work on specific projects where CSO engagement is planned.
- Conduct procurement and contract management training.
- Ensure that CSO engagement is timed for maximum impact, and that flexibility is built into the contracts with CSOs.
- Assist DMCs to create measures for performance-based selection of CSOs through performance audits, transparency, and accountability measures, among others.
- Assist DMCs to develop systems and processes to finance and sustain ongoing CSO engagement.
- Conduct knowledge-sharing and engagement events between the proposed implementing agency and identified CSOs, to sensitize each other to processes and personnel.
- Be a supervising consultant during project implementation, to act as a bridge between the implementing agencies and the CSO partners, especially at the early stages of project implementation.

As a support to the facility, SARD will perform the following:

- Consult with CSOs and government partners for projects with significant scope for CSO engagement at the design phase.
- Organize roadshows (physically or online) to orient CSOs on pipeline projects with CSO participation.
- Prepare materials to support CSO engagement that will explain ADB and government's expectations from CSOs and their contributions to the project and the support that CSOs can call on to prepare project plans and budgets and in strengthening relations with government partners.
- Seek feedback on CSO and government's experiences in project engagement and the support and assistance needed in the long term.

---

1   See Part 4 Due Diligence, Procurement, and Partnerships from p. 55 onward, in ADB. 2021. *A Sourcebook for Engaging with Civil Society Organizations in Asian Development Bank Operations*. Manila.

www.ingramcontent.com/pod-product-compliance
Lightning Source LLC
Chambersburg PA
CBHW061221270326
41926CB00032B/4804